"I highly recommend *The Competitive Parent* to all parents and coaches of young football players. Young football players will truly benefit from programs implementing what is written in this outstanding book."

—Ron Chamberlain, Ph. D.
Sports Psychologist

"I have counseled thousands of top athletes and worked closely with their parents and coaches. Christopher Tateo has written an informative and useful book for kids, parents, and coaches who are seriously involved with football."

—Jay P. Grant, Ph.D., Psychotherapist
Founder of stayinthezone.com

"I found *The Competitive Parent* extremely uncomplicated in outlining all aspects of coaching youth athletes who are entering football. Every youth football coach should follow this comprehensive recipe for successful coaching."

—Edward Palmer, Author of *Getting Started Sports Books*

"Chris Tateo has written an important book for anyone interested in coaching youth football. Every coach today has to face the dilemma of winning versus other goals, and that is why every coach should read this book to learn the proper values and to hear them championed by a young coach passionate about them."

—Fred Northup
President, Athletes for a Better World

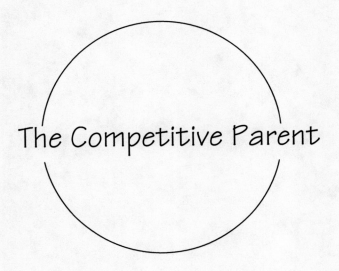

The Competitive Parent

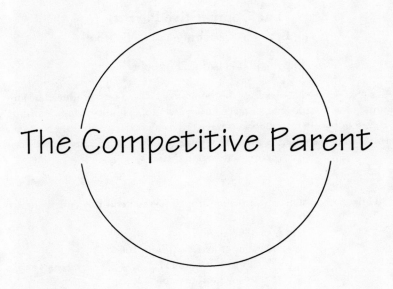

The Competitive Parent

The Ethics of Coaching Youth Football

Christopher Tateo

iUniverse, Inc.
New York Lincoln Shanghai

The Competitive Parent
The Ethics of Coaching Youth Football

Copyright © 2007 by Christopher Tateo

iUniverse books may be ordered through booksellers or by contacting:

iUniverse
2021 Pine Lake Road, Suite 100
Lincoln, NE 68512
www.iuniverse.com
1-800-Authors (1-800-288-4677)

ISBN: 978-0-595-40246-5 (pbk)
ISBN: 978-0-595-84622-1 (ebk)

Printed in the United States of America

Contents

About the Coach

Growing up, football meant everything to me. It kept me out of trouble, gave me direction, and helped me make friends. Football taught me about relationships and creativity. It gave me a work ethic I've carried with me all my life.

Now my football career has come full circle. I started at the Pee Wee level as a player. Now I'm in my ninth year of coaching it. I can honestly tell you that coaching has been the best experience I've ever had. There is nothing more satisfying than molding young kids into football players—and, more important, into young men.

Growing up, I wasn't the biggest kid, but I learned to play football with great confidence. I learned to conquer my fears and found a way to use my size to my advantage. My trademark as a player was my great work ethic; I had the endurance to give 100 percent effort on every play—an ability my bigger peers couldn't challenge. This ethic led me to many Pee Wee, Midget, high-school, and college achievements. Throughout my journey, I learned that football was more a game of strategy than a game of brute force.

My glory days may be over, but my heart still lives for football. I apply the same energy to coaching that I did to playing. I'm presently coaching my old childhood football team—the same one that once learned very little while enduring the screaming and yelling of my old coach. From those old youth-football days, I still carry with me a philosophy that I gained as a kid struggling to understand football: I told myself back then that if the coach would only show us more compassion and patience, we would probably learn more about the game. I wish he'd just taken me aside and said, "Chris, this is how it's done."

Who would have thought that years later, I'd have the chance to be that understanding coach? I've coached youth football successfully over the years because I can put myself in the shoes of these kids who are just starting out in football. I know what it's like to fear the hits. I know what it's like to doubt your own abilities and lack self-esteem. As their coach, I'm these kids' biggest fan and greatest motivator. I help them play to the best of their ability. My wife and I often are asked when we're going to have children. My response is, "I have thirty kids a year. How many more do I need?"

HOW AM I QUALIFIED TO WRITE THIS BOOK?

Experience wrote this book. I had no blueprint to follow when I first started coaching. I had plenty of experience playing football, but none coaching it. I thought youth football would be easy to handle. I thought I could make the practices fun and the players would listen to everything I said. Boy, was I wrong!

I had a horrific first four years as an assistant coach. Learning the hard way, I slowly came to understand the dos and don'ts of coaching youth football. Keeping tabs on the needs of youth-football players is amazingly tough: who's crying, who's fighting, who's fooling around, who's not paying attention, who's not playing, who's got a cut, who's sick, who's not coming to practice, who's late … it goes on and on. Youth-league coaches must wear many hats: director, doctor, lawyer, politician, equipment manager, and field crew.

I know this book will serve you well as a blueprint to successful youth-league coaching. You can be a hard-nosed coach, but you can do it in an enlightening way. Give your players the attention they need, and they will know what you expect from them. Management is the key to successful practices and games. Keep everyone in line and on the same page. Keep practices flowing, fun, and productive. Last, take everything with a grain of salt. Problems will always occur. Don't let them get you down, Coach! Remember, I'm always behind you.

Coach Chris Tateo

Introduction

This book is filled with cutting-edge ideas that will help parents and coaches prepare for practices, teach efficiently, create drills, and inspire players to be productive. Many instructional coaching books on the market diagram plays and illustrate how to plan games, but few teach coaches how to prepare the minds of young football players for this modern-day gladiator sport.

Coaching and preparing young players is vastly different from coaching teens and young adults in high school or college. Children are more mentally and physically fragile; they need a positive role model who will prepare them for competition. Inexperienced coaches and parents can do more harm than good in developing a child's esteem. The old-school coaching method of yelling, screaming, and pulling on a player's facemask is over.

The following chapters will help coaches and parents deal with the intangibles surrounding youth football. I know parents have busy lives, but over the past few years, volunteer coaches for youth sports have become hard to find. Parents may find coaching to be a great recreational activity that can really help young people.

Yes, coaching can be like taking on another job, but this book will give you the ideas, tips, and communication skills to make your coaching experience enjoyable. This straightforward book will help you to be more productive in your coaching. You will learn to minimize your hardships, making coaching a personal achievement that you'll remember for a lifetime.

MILLION-DOLLAR BABY

Let's do a reality check before we go any further. There are many delusional parents out there who bank on their child's future as a professional football player. In truth, the chance of receiving a Division I scholarship is slim, and professional football employs only the elite of the elite.

At the professional level, football is more than just a game—it's a business. Professional teams spend millions of dollars scouting, evaluating, scrutinizing, testing, and retesting recruits to find players who will be assets to their organiza-

xiv   The Competitive Parent

tion. General managers, scouts, and coaches put their jobs on the line each season, striving to find these players.

Professional football players are natural athletes, born with uncanny physical size and speed. The key words are "size" and "speed": professional teams look for those attributes in an athlete. Exceptional height and speed cannot be taught or learned. To even be considered by a professional football team, an athlete must be big (six feet three inches tall) or fast (with a forty-yard-dash time of under 4.4 seconds). Professional teams take that raw potential and then invest their time in shaping the recruit into a professional player.

The reason I bring this subject up is that every year I meet parents who are entrenched in their child's athletic career. The stress these parents put on their kids is horrifying. Parents should worry about the child's education first; if the child has the talent to move on to the college or professional ranks, fate will take care of it. Parents should view football (and all youth sports) as their child's outlet for releasing the stress of everyday activities—not turn football into a source of yet more stress for their child.

One

Thinking about Coaching Youth Football

If you have no experience with football in any way, I suggest you begin with a secondary role in coaching a youth team. Find someone who has coaching experience to be the head coach. You can have the responsibilities of being an assistant coach in training to be a future head coach. Football is a very complex sport; extensive knowledge of technique and fundamentals is necessary to get players ready for the game. An inexperienced coach is also a safety hazard; when done incorrectly, practice drills can be dangerous. I would say that 90 percent of injuries happen at practice, not in games.

Taking an assistant position doesn't mean you won't have a major role in the players' development. Assistant coaches can run drills and even sub in if the head coach is absent. Assistant coaches can specialize as position coaches, such as a defensive-line coach or as a coordinator of a specific unit, such as a special teams. Specializing allows a coach to concentrate on one area of football, where he or she can really excel.

Find time to go to your local high-school or college football practices. There you can broaden your ideas on how to teach kids' football the right way. Coaching strategies are always evolving. High-school and college coaches usually have years of experience; observe what they are teaching their players. You can gain a wealth of knowledge just by watching practices. I would even suggest approaching the coach for some advice on techniques and strategies. Explain that you're a volunteer for the local youth-football team. Coaches may be more willing to give you pointers if they know they'll be getting your players in future years.

Paying your dues

Your first year as a coach may be very difficult. Even a veteran coach hosting a new crop of beginners can have a tough year. I hope you're not one of those gung ho dads or Sunday armchair quarterbacks determined to coach a Pee Wee or Midget team to a championship season; I wish you luck, but the odds are small. Even if you have experience playing football or coaching at a higher level, youth football is unique. The rules are different, and the weights, the skills, and the young minds of your players are all different. It takes time—sometimes years—to adjust to all these obstacles. Losing games doesn't help the situation either. Losing brings out the worst in people. I've been there, and I know the helpless feeling. Losing coaches find themselves arguing with referees and parents ... and as often as not getting hostile with their players. It's tough! I just want to prepare you for the worst.

Yes, the experience of coaching does get better over time, but if you really want to win games and enjoy the experience of coaching, you'll have to pay your dues. Experience is the key to enjoying coaching at the youth level—and to winning. Experience means participating in your youth league for two or three years. Learn the offensive and defensive strategies of youth football. Learn through game experiences, and from taking notes on what the most successful teams in your league do. Soon enough you'll learn from your mistakes, experiences, and surroundings. Over time you will naturally adjust your coaching behavior and skills. Your practices will change, your attitude will change, and you'll get more creative in designing your offensive and defensive schemes. The next thing you know, you'll be winning—and building relationships in the process. You'll be relaxed, confident, and proud to be coaching your youth-football team.

Do I have the patience to coach kids?

Communication is key to teaching young football players. Coaching at this level takes a lot of patience. You cannot yell at your players in anger; this approach will only cause kids to break down psychologically. A good, experienced coach evaluates his or her players and studies each individual's skills.

Over the years, I've seen some horrific episodes in which coaches hollered at, degraded, and physically abused players. Some of these kids are just beginning their football careers. Aggressive, inexperienced coaches will only cause kids to withdraw and rebel, and will ultimately cause damage to their self-esteem. You have to remember that sports builds character, helping children succeed. These kids will later strive to be doctors, lawyers, contractors ... people from all walks of life.

In the short time you have to coach your team, you're going to experience the fear, pain, and tears your little ones will go through. You'll see them share playful smiles with friends. You'll be there for their first touchdown celebration. You'll see emotions in your players that their own parents have probably never seen.

The goal is always to lift a child's spirit. Give them an identity. Show that you care about them. Guide them through the basics of football. Groom them to have great sportsmanship, win or lose.

Coaching your own child

If you're taking on the challenge of coaching youth football, you probably have a son or daughter on the roster. It is important that you explain to your child before the season begins that your behavior will be different on the football field than it would be at home. Your child will have to understand that they won't be the center of attention at practice or in a game. A coach must give attention to and care for all his or her players. When you're at home, you can be the parent you've always been. You can even practice some football skills at home, where your son or daughter can get plenty of attention, on days when no practice is scheduled.

Place players into positions carefully. Don't make the mistake of penciling your child in for all the glory positions if he or she hasn't earned it. Let your child earn the role; your fairness will go a long way toward gaining the confidence of your child's teammates. The last thing you want is animosity from players or parents who feel that you are biased. Your child's physical skills will prove they earned the spot, with no questions asked.

Of course, a bias in the opposite direction is just as detrimental. Over the years, I've seen some coaches bash their own children more than the other players on the team, just because they feel the child is underachieving. Some coaches believe they are giving their child an advantage over the others because they are in control of the team, and some feel they can use that control to push their child to stardom. Encouraging your son or daughter to do better is fine, but anger or harsh criticism is likely to frighten your child—and everyone else. If you are prone to these reactions, it may be more beneficial for your assistant coaches to coach your child in different aspects of the game to avoid ongoing confrontations. If you just can't keep yourself from being your child's biggest critic, I recommend that you hang up your clipboard and let someone else coach the team. Football should be a fun and exciting time for both the parent and child.

Winning isn't everything

Anyone who enjoys sports has the competitive desire to win. When you're the coach, your competitive pride is even more magnified, because the team's achievements (or lack thereof) reflect your personal work. In your mind, a series of losses may mean that you're not a very good coach. This kind of thinking is nonsense.

This is what separates youth football from other levels of coaching: these are young players taking baby steps into organized football. You need to accept the imperfections that come with this age group: fundamentals, penalties, and losses. You are a coach—a mentor who will provide discipline while guiding players through the experience of this magnificent sport. The greatest lessons that your team can learn will come through losses.

Life is not perfect. There will always be mistakes, bad decisions, and situations you have no control over. We can only dust ourselves off, learn from our experiences … and then try again.

Two

The Season Approaches

Your first few weeks as a coach may be overwhelming as you get yourself situated in your new role. You will probably start by attending some league meetings and studying the game rule book during the summer months. Then, as the season arrives, you'll have the honor of fielding parents' questions about signing up, practices, and game schedules.

Then, finally, the first day of camp will begin as you greet your troops. A well-planned stretching and conditioning program should be in place for that first week of camp. After a few weeks of leading your players through conditioning, you will need to organize and distribute equipment. Finally you will need to evaluate your players and pencil them into positions. These are some of the areas of youth football that you'll have to sort out as a coach, and plenty more will spring up on you. With some detailed planning and organization, you'll find ways to minimize these minor headaches and get into what you want to do most: coach.

Team parents

Some of the players' parents will seek opportunities to help out. A **team parent** can be valuable to a coach. A team parent can keep the other parents informed of meetings, schedule changes, and team functions. This type of assistance takes a great deal of pressure off the coaches. Coaches can concentrate on preparing the players for games without outside distractions. Team parents can coordinate with other parents by phone chain or e-mail to notify them of any upcoming events. Team parents can also serve as middlemen between parents and coaches when either side has a concern about a child's well-being. A coach can accommodate parents' concerns before a confrontation occurs.

In the long run, communication among parents makes the football experience more enjoyable for coaches, kids, and the football community.

Assembling a coaching staff

It will be necessary to put a small coaching staff together. Youth leagues around the country practice three times a week and requires lots of preparation time, so time management is important. There's offense, defense, special teams, and individual drills to go through. It's also nice to have extra eyes and ears on the field; kids can wander like cattle on the Texas plains during practice sessions. It's up to you, cowboy, to round them up and be productive with the short time you have each week.

Assistant coaches can help divide the team into small groups to work on individual drills. They can help with players who are lagging behind or watch for slackers. Assistant coaches can give you updates on how players are performing, and perhaps provide advice on how to enhance that performance. Assistant coaches can take stress off you when you are having a rough day. Give your assistants some responsibility, so you can sit back, relax, collect your thoughts, and have some fun with the kids. Most importantly, an assistant coach can fill in when you're unable to make practice. They'll be familiar with your system and should fill it nicely.

If you do put a staff together, try to find some friends to be your assistants. Friends can offer an unbiased point of view if they have no relationships with the players on the team. Having friends as staff members will allow the coaches to communicate their feelings openly, so that biases and conflicting egos will not get in the way of decision making when it comes to the team.

More often than not, another parent will assist you on the sidelines. Be conscious that there are other players on the team besides your own. Also be aware that parents will be ready to pounce if a coach favors his or her own children and neglects the rest of the players on the team. Make sure you screen assistant candidates thoroughly. Ask if they have any experience coaching children. Ask if they have any experience playing or coaching football. Sometimes, just by observing the person's mannerisms, you can get a feel of how good they are with kids. Always be sure that you have a director or president of the league involved with the approval process. This is important, because if anything goes awry with the new assistant, you can then work out the issue in a forum.. Whomever you choose to be your assistant coach, make sure it is someone who has the same passion for football as you do. Find someone who cares about the players as if they were his or her own.

It all begins at boot camp

Coaches needs to be in total control of their teams. If you don't focus on discipline, structure, and organization from the first day of practice, you will have less time for game planning and preparing your players for battle. Keep in mind that it's natural for kids to have short attention spans; they love to mess around and spark their own interests.

Now, I'm not suggesting you be a drill sergeant; there's no need to yell at the kids as if they're in the army. Be strict, but drill your youngsters with kindness and tough love. Coaches must model appropriate behavior to get that behavior from players in return: paying attention, behaving, working hard, and improving skills. Young football players learn by mimicking those around them. The manner in which you act and communicate at practice and in games is one your football players will adopt themselves. If coaches are sloppy in teaching, then their players will be sloppy. If coaches are organized, then their players will be prepared. If coaches yell at referees, their players will think it's all right to do the same.

Every coach's goal, at every level of football, is an organized group of players who take direction well and work for the good of the team. The way to achieve this with young football players is to praise positive work habits. When players are working hard and giving effort, reward them with kind words of praise. Use praise wisely; don't encourage players who gave little effort. Let those unpraised players mimic the players who are striving to get better. Call attention to players' strengths—especially players who are less physically gifted or persistent. Kids love praise, and they feed off it no matter who it comes from. Your praise should reflect your emphasis on discipline and organization. Your players will begin to respect you and follow your direction, because they believe that you truly care about their interests and well-being. Carefully chosen praise is what leads a football team to a successful season.

Communicating with your players

There will be frustrating times when your players don't do what you ask or don't understand the concept you're trying to get across to them. These are the times you will need to collect yourself. Use all your tools as a coach to either demonstrate a concept or illustrate it visually so the kids will understand.

Losing your temper and talking down to kids is an ingredient for disaster, especially for seven- to twelve-year-olds. Kids today are influenced by television, music, and video games. Kids want to grow up early. You will learn that kids have their limits and will respond to anger or harsh criticism by shutting down, purposely ignoring, or disobeying your direction. Kids in youth football are at an age where they are beginning to develop their own personalities and seek identity among their peers. If you belittle a kid at practice, the negative impact will filter throughout the whole team. You will intimidate your players, and they will be afraid to do anything wrong. You'll create an atmosphere that will make learning tough.

Treat kids like adults. Talk to them like adults. Tell them what you want. Speak to them in a mellow tone. Encourage them even when they make mistakes.

If you have a kid who is disruptive, try not to be confrontational. Disarm the player with friendliness. Find the problem. Try to solve the problem, and don't take it more seriously than necessary. Communication with your players benefits you as well as them.

Taking control of your practices

Consistently structuring practices is important right from the first session. Coaches need to be in control of their practice sessions. Your weekly time frame for conditioning and preparing your players for a game will be minimal. Practices during the week need to flow smoothly if you are going to accomplish everything on your agenda. It will be only a matter of time until players choose to misbehave or get lazy on you.

I've perfected one way to add discipline and structure to my practices. I call it **the countdown**. Whenever my players drag their feet, I count down from five to one, as if the seconds were expiring off the game clock. If the kids aren't where they're supposed to be when their time is up, they must line up for some short wind sprints as a mild punishment.

Believe me, your kids will learn quickly that you mean business, and rarely will you have a problem with players dragging their feet in practice. Be consistent, so they know you mean what you say. Do not abuse your power by forcing players to do wind sprints for long periods of time, or you'll create harsh feelings among your team. Two or three sprints are enough to get your point across. Always make it a point to explain why the team is running. Explain that it's nothing personal; the team just has a lot of work to do, and players must maintain an upbeat pace to get everything in.

The countdown philosophy will also prepare kids for an actual game situation. I have often used a hurry-up offense at the end of games when we were behind on points. My players were conditioned to line up at the line of scrimmage, play after play, with no huddle.

Three

Getting Everyone in the Game

In youth sports, playing time has always been the biggest concern among parents. Any parent expects their child to see some playing time. This is by far the biggest obstacle for coaches also. The challenge of finding chemistry and competitiveness among the shuffle of players is enormously stressful. Careful planning can give you leverage to balance the level of talent on your team. Begin your planning by choosing a first string, a second string, and possibly even a third string. The typical pecking order will put your most productive players on the first string, with others following on the second and third strings.

I recommend that you keep the team competitive by mixing some productive players with some inexperienced players. Mixing talent allows you to cover up for players who may still be shy of contact in games. This will give them valuable experience that will help them build confidence in themselves and encourage them to believe that they can play with their more athletic peers. Most inexperienced players feel more comfortable playing next to more aggressive veteran teammates. They may feel secure having experienced players picking up the slack on the field. By observing the action up close, inexperienced athletes just might break out of their shells and become more productive themselves.

It is much easier to rotate players into a game for defense than for offense. Defense is instinctive; all the player has to do is be aggressive and tackle! It's more difficult to rotate offensive players, because good offense requires more technique and strategic blocking schemes—and there's also a snap count to remember.

Dealing with two-sport athletes

Some players on your roster may participate in a conflicting sport during football season. These two-sport players are bound to miss practices during the week—and perhaps even some games.

I truly believe that these children should choose one sport or the other, for many reasons.

- Participating in two sports will physically and mentally wear a child down. Kids will be sluggish in practice, and they will be more susceptible to injury from the physical workload.

- Consider the child's schoolwork: how can a child have the mental capacity to do homework after a double load of practices during the week?

- These players' inability to attend all practices and games is unfair to the rest of the players on the team, who are fighting for playing time.

- Making up for the two-sport athlete's missed practices adds enormous stress to a coach's job; each time these players miss a practice, the coach has to repeat the lessons they missed. A coach also has to wonder whether the player has enough mental focus to absorb the new material being taught.

- Uncertainty about whether a player will show up for each game can cause the rest of the team to lose trust in that player.

It's very hard for a coach to tell a player to pick one sport when the season has already begun. It would be worth your while to have a written statement on the registration form. If a player is participating in two sports in the same season, you can discuss with the parents the issues that may arise. Most times it's not the parents who are to blame for the conflict; it's the children who badger their parents to allow them to diversify, because their friends are doing it also.

Minimizing jealousy between players

Place your players into positions early. This will stop any bickering among the kids. The rules of the league are usually a big help in this decision. There are weight restrictions for offensive linemen, defensive linemen, ball carriers, linebackers, and secondary players on defense. Smaller players will naturally be at the skilled positions, and larger players will be designated as anchors to the offensive and defensive lines. Some advice, though: regardless of size, you might want to put your best athletes on the offensive line to block, or the defensive line to penetrate. My advice is to fill important positions, such as quarterback, by evaluating players based on their knowledge of the game, maturity, and aggressiveness. Forget about passing and receiving drills to find positions for these kids.

Two areas that cannot be measured are heart and focus. No matter their ability, kids who give maximum effort consistently are blessings to a coach. These are the players you love to coach; they inspire not only you, but the entire team. One reason I return to coaching each year is the enjoyment of seeing how the human spirit lives in some of these kids. Even at their young age, they have an amazing level of fight and passion for the game of football. It makes you proud to be a coach!

Dealing with parents

Parents are always going to have concerns about their children. You will field a variety of questions regarding everything from equipment malfunctions to practice schedules. Always be polite and courteous to parents. Sometimes they can be your greatest asset in motivating players. Playing minutes are, by far, most parents' greatest concern. All parents will want to see their child get just as many game minutes as the other players on the team. Parents sometimes don't realize how complex football can be. You cannot just put a child in a game the way you can in baseball, soccer, or basketball. Players must prepare for contact and remember their assignments. Players need to be alert physically and mentally for the collisions they will be susceptible to on any given play. Players who are fragile in size, lacking in skills, or short on experience cannot be thrown to the wolves in the game of football.

Other players, because of their lack of effort and horsing around during practice, simply haven't earned the playing minutes that others receive. Players who distract others at practice should not be rewarded with quality playing time. How do you explain to parents that their children are not the angels they had thought? Obviously this is not easy.

I've had to call several parents and explain that their child has to pick up the pace in learning or participating if he or she wants quality playing time. Some of these kids just hide in the back of lines in practice or show no commitment to getting better. There's not much a coach can do but to encourage these players and share concerns with their parents.

Fielding a large roster

There is a misconception among youth-football coaches that fielding a large roster, made up of thirty or forty kids, is a benefit to the coach. Yes, you can pick from a pool of talent to make up the best team possible, and you can run full intersquad scrimmages at practices during the week to give kids valuable game experience. But in the long run, the rewards do not outweigh the headaches of carrying a large roster of young football players.

For one, youth coaches are too understaffed to effectively teach and control this many players. Maintaining the football equipment necessary for such a large roster can be a hassle. The large number of parents means more questions to field. But by far the greatest and most stressful drawback of a large roster is the challenge of substituting kids into a game. In most youth-football leagues around the country, it is mandatory that every player participate in a game for x number of plays. If this doesn't happen, you will hear about it from players, parents, and league officials.

Fielding a large roster of players is great for a high-school or college coach who has a large coaching staff and can pick and choose from a lottery of mature talent. The rest of the players can simply be cut from the team. In youth football, there is no such thing as cutting kids from a team.

Here are some other issues to be aware of when fielding a large roster of kids. Plan ahead to solve these problems:

- It is very hard to work with players individually. If you give one player attention, the rest of the team will find time to horse around.

- With a large roster, you'll have at least two players who need help with their equipment at the beginning of practice. This is valuable time spent away from the team.

- Kids can be aware that coaches are outnumbered at times; some players will see this as an opportunity to goof around. Kids will find time to talk during practice, in drills, and at the end of lines.

Making an A team and a B team

If you have a large roster of kids, I think it is very important to form a first and second string. The second-string team will include first-year players and players who need improvement. Of course, with more players, you will need more coaches. Your coaching staff will teach the second string the same plays and techniques as the first group. This way, when second-string players progress and make strides, they can easily be put into the game with the first-string players. The other benefit of forming two teams is the excellent practice scrimmages. On game day, such an arrangement allows you to substitute the entire first unit for the second unit, which allows you to get your whole roster in the game. By forming a first and second string, you essentially create an in-house system for player improvement.

Undoubtedly, some parents will take offense that their child is on the second string. It is very important that you have a preseason orientation with the parents as a group. Explain the safety issues and the learning curve that kids have to meet to be fair to everyone. Everyone is going to play. Children who work harder than others, who are disciplined and well behaved, will see more playing time, because they deserve it. The other players will have to meet that criteria week in and week out.

Now, everything is out in the open. All parents and players know what the coaches expect from them. Let's get on with the season.

Four

Evaluating Player Talent

In this chapter I will give you advice on how to get the most information about your players. Having information about your players' physical attributes, and personality will go a long way in helping you teach your players the game of football. You never want to clash with your players with silly arguments. You also do not want to offend players who are very sensitive to criticism. Coaches and players have to work together to be successful in learning and winning games. Above all we want this to be a great experience for yourself and the children.

Gathering Information from Parents

You will probably meet and greet parents early in the preseason. Use this time to get to know your players. It's nice to know something about your players before you even get on the practice field. Be productive when asking parents about their children's athletic experience. Ask simple questions:

- Does the child have knowledge of the game?
- Does he or she watch football on television?
- Do the parents have any football experience at all?
- Does the child have experienced older siblings?
- Is the child active in other sports? (This will give you an idea of any useful skills they may have gained in other sports, such as hockey or lacrosse. You might even get an idea of what position they can compete for: A pitcher on a baseball team might be a good quarterback. A lacrosse player might be a good running back because of his or her coordination and toughness.)

By asking parents these questions, you are showing that you care and are interested in their child's well-being. This conversation can help you quickly develop a bond with the player and parent.

Avoiding spoiling kids early on

Practices that offer too much fun too fast can spoil children. This may sound funny, but it's true. Don't make practice too fun the first week or two. Focus instead on conditioning and evaluating talent to fill open positions that you may have. I once made the huge mistake of spoiling kids with fun drills the opening week of football practices. I made the mistake of having the players participate in a lot of fun passing drills early, which gave the players the impression that they were all going to be wide receivers, as in two-hand touch football. Allowing kids to get into a hyper state may prompt false expectations; kids will think every practice will be fun and lighthearted. Practices like this will ultimately cause coaches to lose control of the team.

I also made the mistake of having my bigger players (potential linemen) participate in receiving and running drills, as running backs would. This gave them the perception that they might have a chance to run the ball in a game. All youth-football leagues have weight restrictions for ball carriers. Running back drills for linemen and other such activities can set up your bigger players for a letdown—which may cause them to lose interest in playing football altogether. However, this doesn't exempt your linemen from participating in ball-handling drills to practice recovering fumbles. Be up-front with your players about weight restrictions, so each family knows beforehand that their child may be over the weight limit to be a ball carrier.

Sometimes coaches create their own monsters. Keep in mind the reason kids join up is to catch the ball like Jerry Rice or run the ball like Emmitt Smith. I don't think they often intend to be blockers!

Evaluating team talent

Evaluating talent can be tough. One thing is for certain: every member of the team must learn how to block and tackle. A player who can do these two things can play any position on the field. Judging talent at the youth level is sometimes trickier than you might think. Yes, you can easily evaluate physical size and skill. But one underestimated criterion is a child's maturity, especially in skilled positions like quarterback. Mature children have control over their emotions. They don't seem to get as nervous as their less mature peers, and they pick up complex material quickly.

Always carry a clipboard with you to keep notes on the strengths and weaknesses of your players as you test their abilities. First, do a series of agility and speed drills to test athletic performance. Second, get an offensive team in a huddle and call a series of plays to see who has good memory skills. Third, place your players on the line of scrimmage in a three-point stance to see who has the discipline to remember a random snap count. Little drills like these will help you measure your players' mental and physical capabilities.

As you will see in the following list, there are many other characteristics to look for when placing talent.

Agility is the ability of players to move in any direction with ease. Agility is crucial in skilled positions like quarterback, running back, and linebacker. You'll also want some agile offensive and defensive linemen. Agile offensive linemen can give your team the ability to "pull" and get in front of your sweeping running backs. They can also release the line of scrimmage and get linebackers downfield. Defensive linemen can use agility to avoid oncoming blockers. They can also chase down ball carriers from behind.

Speed is key. Your fastest players will usually play the skilled positions of quarterback, running back, and defensive secondary. Fast players can run the ball outside on offense. They can be a deep-pass threat. They can return punts, and they can chase ball carriers down on breakaway runs.

Height is a good feature in a player. Tall players are great for playing tight end on offense and defense end on defense. At the youth level, tall tight ends always give you the option to pass. I loved designing quick passes, right over the defensive line. A quick, short pass can put the defense back on their heels. A good combination is a tall quarterback connecting with a tall tight end. The odds of a completion are very much in your favor. Tall players can also be great defensive ends. The height and arm reach of these players can contain a ball carrier sweeping to the outside. Tall defensive ends can also be intimidating for the offensive team, because they seem to force the action inside the tackles.

Players with plenty of confident **aggressiveness** can play anywhere on the field. They usually have no fear. They can run the ball and block, and they make great linebackers. Be careful, though—some players can get out of control, falling out of position to make a play on the field.

Full equipment evaluation

After observing the conditioning sessions of your equipment-free players the first couple of weeks, you might have chosen some athletic kids to fill open positions. You were probably impressed by these players' speed, agility, and attitude.

The story changes when the pads go on. The tight, distracting equipment makes a big difference. The crashing of helmets seems to dim the once-upbeat attitude of your players. The speed and aggressiveness seem to fade. For most players, full contact is all new. You'll know right away by the players' body language whether they are looking forward to some contact. Ease your players into contact.

Over a few weeks, you can observe players and decide which can fill an open position on the offensive and defensive side of the ball. Kids who have played football before can sometimes adjust to the equipment and prepare themselves for full-contact football relatively quickly. Other players will have to ease into full contact. At the beginning of training camp, limit your players' protective gear to helmets for the first week. Add shoulder pads for the second week. By the third or fourth week, your players should be ready for full gear.

Misled players

Children seem to be conditioned at a young age to value the attention their heroes receive on television. Most of your players have at one time or another pretended to hit the game-winning home run or catch the touchdown pass. Deflecting kids' attention away from the glorified positions they see their heroes play is a tough part of coaching. Year after year, I see kids wanting to be quarterbacks, running backs, receivers, and linebackers. Kids want the attention of making a touchdown or sacking the quarterback for a loss.

It's important for you to explain that every position on the team is crucial to success. Every position can be fun if you make it that way. If kids are going to enjoy football and contribute to the team, they must broaden their minds. They must add value to their position in order to feel that powerful sense of accomplishment they desire. If players value attention, then they must give attention to their position. If their position calls for them to block, then they need to make the greatest block they possibly can. If their position requires them to play nose tackle on the defensive line, then they need to make a great tackle. The old saying, "To get attention, you must give attention," definitely applies to youth football: players must give attention to the position they are assigned. If they do that to the best of their ability, people will notice.

The David-versus-Goliath theory

The majority of your players will be small in stature. You'll also have a minority of players who are blessed with physical attributes (height, weight) that are favorable for football. It is easy to motivate larger kids to dominate smaller kids, because of their sheer strength and power.

You'll have to encourage your smaller players to offset the size advantage of other players by generating power by their own physical means. Smaller players can generate power using quickness and speed. The more momentum (speed) a smaller player can generate, the more he or she can offset the size of the larger, stronger opponent. Here are some instances where a smaller player can offset size with speed.

- A smaller offensive lineman against a larger defensive lineman: a quick "charge" out of the offensive player's stance will neutralize a bigger opponent at the line of scrimmage.

- Smaller running backs performing a downfield block on linebackers: a running back sprinting at full speed will offset the size of larger linebacker.

- Defensively, a smaller player would need to generate momentum to tackle a larger ball carrier on impact.

Five

Productive Practices

Football games are won in practice. What you do in a practice is what you'll do in a game. Preparation and getting your players ready both physically and mentally are ingredients for success. At practice a coach can be creative in game planning—and moving personnel around, if need be. Players used to burn bridges with me by missing practice, because every practice is meaningful in preparing players for the position they may be playing in an upcoming game.

Scheduling practices effectively

Practice scheduling is the key to efficiently running a practice with the little time you have. Without good scheduling, you can easily lose track of time. Practices at the youth level usually last about an hour and a half, sometimes two hours. In all my years of coaching, this has never seemed to be enough time to go over everything thoroughly.

Be organized and prepared. Take time during the week to write down what you want to work on. It could be a new play, a new drill, or just preparation for the next game. Keep practices upbeat and moving forward with strong momentum. Move from drill to drill and play to play. I have always believed that a smooth pace is necessary for a good practice. This means no interruptions and no horsing around.

Pacing your practices is especially important, because football is naturally interactive for kids; they're in a fun atmosphere, away from their parents. A brisk practice pace will not give players time to talk. They will be more attentive and easier to handle. Your organization helps build your image as a coach in control of your team—a coach who is preparing them well for football games.

Bonding with your players

I believe that to have a successful season, coaches must form a special relationship with their players. One of the obstacles to achieving this bond is the defensive barrier that many kids have when they first come to practice.

Here's some advice: When meeting your players for the first time, shake their hands and engage in the typical introduction pleasantries. Be sure that in every practice after that, you remember each child's first name. This technique always makes the child feel more comfortable.

Kids are naturally shy and defensive about themselves. It's important that coaches show that they care about their players. Show your players that they are not just another number on the team. A good relationship with your players will make coaching much easier. From time to time, show them your softer side by talking with them about interests outside football. Believe me, it's better to have a child approach you with a problem than to hear about it from his or her parent. Make yourself very accessible to your players. Don't refuse to participate in practical jokes or occasional horsing around. It's this playful environment that creates bonds between players and coaches.

Unifying your team

It's important to start the team-bonding process on the first day of practice. Give your veteran players the assignment of big brother. Explain to them that they are role models to the younger guys. These experienced players should encourage their younger teammates whenever it is needed. Putting trust in your veterans gives them an incentive to be good leaders on the field. With this commitment, you gain a more organized, disciplined, and productive team.

Encourage the younger guys to learn from their older teammates. They can watch and mimic what the veterans do. This advice and the introduction to veteran players always seems to put the new kids at ease. Their anxiety about meeting new people and being judged can be put to rest.

It's important that the team works as a unit in practice and in games.

Creating a positive practice environment

A coach should always come to practice with a positive attitude. Everyone has a bad day from time to time, but do not come to practice to let your frustrations out on vulnerable children. For me, practice was my sanctuary; during the week,

I couldn't wait to get my mind on something productive and fun, like coaching football. But sometimes I've dealt with the combination of a bad day at work and players fooling around at practice. You just have to think before you react. You cannot allow seven- to eleven-year-olds to stress you out and ruin the rest of your day. Enjoy coaching as your getaway. How many chances do you have to become a kid again? You're in control of the environment; you can make it fun and enjoyable, or you can become a dictator.

Great coaches are master motivators who fill players with positivity and build their self-esteem. The result is more interest in and effort toward improvement on the football field. Words are your most powerful tool, especially if they are positive. Always find words to compliment your young players. Use phrases such as "great job," or "great effort." High fives and handshakes should fill your practices.

It is especially important to give positive feedback to kids who are not too athletic or popular among their peers. A great comment to make is, "I love the effort; we just have to improve on your technique a little." This way you can focus on what still needs work without breaking kids down. You're giving them a base to improve on. Positive feedback shows your appreciation for your player's work ethic. During each practice, you will observe player improvement fueled by your positive words.

Rewards and incentives for hardworking players

Reward your players who have been working hard, even if they are not as physically skilled as other players on the team. If they have been improving and have developed a good work ethic, they should be rewarded with some valuable time on the playing field. I know that, as coaches, we can stereotype players because they look small or seem clumsy, but you may be surprised if you give them a chance.

Sometimes coaches dread putting these kids in the game for long periods of time, expecting those players to hurt the team's chances of winning the game. With careful planning, you can get these kids in a game without disrupting the chemistry of your team. For example, there are two tight end positions on the offensive line where kids can play for a series of downs and be effective. A formation with two tight ends will allow inexperienced players to play without being in harm's way. Calling quick-run plays up the middle of the field will isolate the play away from these inexperienced players. Young tight ends can build their confidence and learn to face guard or block their defenders outward, away from the play.

Using little incentives like offering playing time as a reward for effort will make your team feel they are a part of something special. Everyone will work hard for one another to execute plays and win games. Never be afraid to have a first, second, third, and even a fourth string of tight ends to rotate during a game. Match up players who will work well together. Give each group a clever name, so they know when to go into the game. For example, I use my Jumbo Team for short-yardage situations.

Team organization

Above everything else you do as a coach, you must make sure your team looks organized, especially on game day. This is showtime; parents are going to evaluate what kind of product you're putting on the field. Forget about winning or losing. How the team looks in terms of kids knowing where to line up and how smoothly the plays are executed will stand out during a game. If there is confusion and sloppy play, it's going to reflect badly on a coach. Yes, this is youth football, but professionalism still matters. You want people to know that you take pride in the team, win or lose. Your team will also get a feeling of confidence knowing they look good both in warm-ups and in the actual game.

Perfection comes from repetition. Practice organization and discipline in practice. Start with stretching, then warm-ups, then offense, then defense, and finally special teams. Explain to your team that sometimes how you look affects how you play.

Humor as a team builder

Throughout this book I preach a lot about being organized, maintaining structure, and keeping kids focused on learning. Practices can be hard, but an occasional laugh or two will balance their tone. Foul-ups and mishaps by coaches and players will lighten your practices from time to time. Teach players by example that it's all right to laugh at their own mistakes. The ability to laugh at themselves allows players to perform freely, making mistakes as they go. Show players there's no reason to get down on themselves. Recognize the mistake, laugh, and get back to improving.

Humor can take focus off a tough coach's practice. Some practical jokes and mishaps can unite a team. Sometimes coaches can even reward hard work with some fun end-of-practice games, such as relay races. Humor also fosters communication, allowing relationships to form between players and coaches. Players will feel more comfortable approaching coaches with problems they're having with football—or anything else on their mind. If you learn anything about coaching football, learn that you need to make youth football fun. Make all that hard work and sacrifice a memorable experience, not a job.

Punishment guidelines

General team discipline and individual punishments are two separate things. I don't believe in strict punishment when your team is horsing around or is not paying attention. Instead, start each practice by sharing the day's agenda with your team. Remind the players that this is their team. Explain to your team that any football coach is only there to organize, teach basic position techniques, and call plays during the game. Coaches do not play in games; the players are responsible for working as a team and executing plays if they want to be successful. Football players should want to be proud of what their team looks like on game day. They don't want to look lost or embarrass themselves when they get out on the field. They want their parents and friends to be in awe of how disciplined and organized they can be as individual players and as a team. It is very important that players listen during the week to achieve these goals.

Warn the team beforehand that if they are disruptive or spaced out, you will wake them up with some team sprints. This message usually gets the kids' attention. Don't give the impression that you're actively seeking out misbehaving players to target. You want your practices to flow smoothly; you don't want your kids to get discouraged or be on edge when they make mistakes.

Hopefully no bad behavior will occur, but if you feel as if you're talking to the wind, then follow through by having the team run three or four sprints from right where they stand. After some running, they'll be too tired to talk or play around. Always have the kids run as a team. Never single out kids for punishment; it will only cause harsh feelings and drain your energy as a coach.

Don't make a big fuss over these interruptions. Tell the team, "You've been working so hard. Why would you want to ruin all that effort?" Explain that the running is nothing personal: "We have a lot of work to do. I need you guys to learn and be productive if you want a successful season."

You're always going to have one overly talkative kid who is disruptive in practice. Find time, either during a water break or after practice, to have a talk. Always disarm children with kindness. Make fun of the situation, and defuse the notion that the player is in trouble. Ask the player to find time before or after practice to converse with friends.

Team-oriented practices

Just as in other sports, it's important to teach good sportsmanship in football, especially among teammates. Players battle each other all practice long, and there are bound to be harsh feelings among the group. I always make it a ritual to have the players high-five and shake hands after intense contact drills. This is to show that practice lessons, no matter how intensely competitive they are, are for the good of the team as a whole, to help each player get better. Practice drills are not designed to see which player can dominate another. Recognition between team-mates really unites a team. Come game day, players will play more productively together, and they'll cheer each other on with more enthusiasm.

Postgame sportsmanship is another area to practice. After some intersquad scrimmages during practice, have the players line up and shake hands as if they were in a real game. If we teach anything as coaches, it is professionalism and sportsmanship. Win or lose, I always made it clear to my team that there is no need for taunting after a game. There's no need for the jawing and chanting; you wouldn't want it done to you, so don't do it to others. Sometimes kids do get overly enthusiastic after a game, so after handshakes I always have my team jog to the farthest corner of the football field, where we can celebrate among ourselves without making the other team feel we are gloating.

Bullies at practice

Through my experiences as a coach, I've formed a theory about bullying: it's always done to the least skillful and least confident kids. Those players get picked on the most. Football practices can be like the African plains sometimes: there are always lions looking for the weak and helpless. If a coach is to keep order in prac-tice, he or she must put a stop to bullying.

First, it's important to give these vulnerable players some confidence. Pull these kids aside and explain to them, "If you show you're weak, they'll always pick on you. Sometimes you have no choice. It's more painful to do nothing than to stand up for yourself."

Bullies seek the feeling of power and dominance. They are usually not bad kids; they just see an opportunity for dominance and take advantage. Try to broaden the minds of the bullying party. Ask them this question: Which feels more powerful, helping others or degrading them? Wouldn't they rather have teammates looking up to them, not despising them? Questions like this will usually prompt a productive response in practice.

Discussing injuries when they occur

Injuries can put a damper on a practice session. An injury can also traumatize the entire team, if it is serious. It's always good idea to sit your players down and talk about the incident. Talk about how it happened and ways to prevent it from happening again. Sometimes injuries happen by accident. Other times kids can be get rowdy with each other. Injuries can really change the mind-set of kids who were once giving 100 percent effort. After an injury, kids may spend most of their time worrying about getting hurt themselves. I suggest you explain to your players that injuries are part of the game; they will happen from time to time. Emphasize that players can minimize injuries by following the coach's directions.

Most injuries you encounter will be minor, but always prepare yourself for the worst. The most common injuries you'll experience are loss of wind, sprains, contusions, and some cuts and scratches. It is prudent that you have a medical kit at every practice. The medical kit should be well stocked, with plenty of bandages and a load of ice packs. It's also a good idea to have a cell phone nearby for emergency calls to parents.

Since a coach is most likely to be in charge when an injury occurs, CPR training should be mandatory. Even if you are already trained in CPR, it's a good idea to brush up on it every year.

Always persuade injured players to come to practice. Most times players can learn just by observing practices. Away from practice, players will tend to lose focus and become reluctant to get back on the football field. Sometimes they will feel that they've let their teammates down by not showing up to practices. Attending practices will build a player's desire to get back on the field.

Safety after practice

When your practices are over, be sure to keep every player in view until their parents have arrived to pick them up. The coach is responsible for their players on the practice field and should extend that responsibility to make sure that every player gets home safely. Have the parents' home-phone and cell-phone numbers handy on your clipboard, so you can give them a call if they are running late. Tell your team that they should be in your sight at all times, and that they should not accept rides with strangers. Even when you have to go somewhere immediately after practice, make sure an assistant coach or parent sticks around until every child is picked up safely.

Six

Making Football Interesting

Most of these kids have never seen football before, let alone played it in an organized environment. Most kids don't know who current NFL players are or the basics of the game. Some kids are playing because their friends are. With this in mind, you must keep your teaching methods simple. Don't assume kids know football terms or the fundamentals of football. Teach your players as if they were made of clay: you're going to have to mold them into football players.

Kids are motivated to learn by interest. So we must keep football interesting and exciting. **Interest equals attention**—the most difficult thing to get from young children. Design some fresh teaching techniques and drills that are game-related. The experience you create with your drills at practice will help kids on game day. Demonstrations, videotape sessions, and fun drills can keep learning fresh. Kids have great imaginations. They can mimic what they see and act out what a coach has scripted for them.

You will notice that players very seldom raise their hands to ask questions. It seems that kids feel foolish asking questions in front of their peers. You should, however, always welcome questions. Questions give coaches feedback on what players need help grasping about the game of football.

Keeping football simple

Kids look to their coach for knowledge. Go into every practice with the assumption that players know very little about the terminology or the basics of the game. Make an effort to explain the rules, techniques, and responsibilities of football. One of the important lessons you can teach a child early on are offensive and defensive formations and alignments. Kids can grasp the concept of how organized football is played. "Offensive formations and defensive alignments" refers to how players are positioned at the line of scrimmage before the ball is snapped. A coach can draw illustrations on a board to demonstrate positioning. Offensively, teams can line up in a wing-T formation, I formation, wishbone, and so on. One basic rule of any formation is that there must be seven players on the line of scrimmage before the ball is snapped.

Defensively, players can be positioned in a 4–4, 4–3, 5–2 alignment before the snap of the ball. In football terms, a 4–4 defense means there are four defensive linemen at the line of scrimmage, with four linebackers behind them for support.

I'm not an advocate of video games for children, but EA Sports's *Madden* series of football games for PlayStation are a fantastic way for kids to learn offensive and defensive formations from the comfort of their homes. These video games give the participants a coaching perspective, allowing them to choose offensive and defensive formations along with some plays to defeat the opponent.

Basic football stances

Offensive and defensive stances are fundamental and must be taught from the first day of practice. Coaches sometimes overlook how important a football stance is to a beginning football player. I've had many kids get confused on which stance to use on offense or defense. It was an area I neglected. I thought kids knew they had to be in a two-point stance to play linebacker.

Yes, coaches do teach the common and most basic offensive three-point stance, but they must also explain a two-point stance, a four-point stance, and their respective uses in a variety of positions on the field. For instance, running backs can be in a two-point stance to give them a better visual of the field before the ball is snapped. Defensive linemen can be in a four-point stance to allow a lower center of gravity to hold their position at line of scrimmage. Linebackers and secondary personnel use a two-point stance to read plays and to ward off any oncoming blockers. Teach these stances to your players early and often. Substitute them in conditioning drills, individual drills, and even warm-ups. A sound football stance is the number-one way to keep children alert before the snap of the ball.

Teaching the rules of the game

Accumulating a lot of penalties can make a team look undisciplined. Players constantly going off sides or holding can make a coach look bad. Discipline can be taught in practice. In the weeks leading up to a game, a coach can demonstrate what holding, off sides, encroachment, and clipping are, so these penalties won't happen in a game. For instance, a coach can work a snap count into any drill or play call to test players, gauging whether players are focused enough to not go off sides. Players will have to take responsibility for themselves, take penalties seriously, and be conscious of the consequences.

Penalties in youth football can be devastating for the offensive team. Gaining any kind of yardage or a first down on offense is an achievement in itself. A penalty of any sort can stall a drive down the field. Instead of a first down and five, an off sides penalty will make it first and fifteen. Catching up will be an uphill battle for any young offensive football team.

Parents and football fans in general want to see a clean and fair football game. Nobody wants to see a team that is prone to penalties or dirty tactics to intimidate the opposing teams. Cursing, punching, spearing, tripping, face-mask pulling, piling on, and late hits should never be tolerated. Any coach allowing this behavior to go on should resign. Make implementing strict guidelines about poor sportsmanship a priority. If deliberate incidents happen in your practice sessions or games, it is time to sit the player down and have a talk with their parents. Allowing dirty play to go on in your practice sessions will ultimately bring your practices into disarray. Players intimidating fellow players with harsh language and unsafe behavior will compromise the team's unity and put players on edge. Players will lose focus, and parents will rightfully complain. I suggest that coaches enforce some strict guidelines before any poor behavior develops.

Demonstrating key concepts

Demonstrations are the most helpful technique a coach can use to teach young players football. Coaches can demonstrate how every position on the football field should be played. Each position has a skill that incorporates footwork, strength, and coordination. A coach can perform these skills and have his or her players mimic those actions immediately. Coaches can also act out how a designed play is supposed to work. It's the acting out of a play or position that gives young kids a visual understanding of how the skill or play is supposed to work. Once they see it, kids can store it in their minds and mimic the action when the situation calls for it. You may have to repeat your demonstrations from practice to practice, so these skills sink into your players' heads, but your players will eventually connect what they experience in practice or a game with what you have shown them. The most gratifying feeling for a coach is seeing a player use a skill that he or she taught them in practice. It shows that all your hard work is paying off.

Another good use of visual aids is the videotaping of some practice sessions, especially on blocking and tackling. A coach can critique the film and help players who are having difficultly. Pick one day out of the week when you can have a film session with the team to go over the fundamentals of blocking and tackling. When players see themselves on film, they can observe what they are doing wrong. When those players get on the practice field again, they can work on improving their technique.

When you demonstrate a skill on the field or critique technique on film, be sure you are knowledgeable in what you are teaching. Even if you have football experience, you should always freshen up on the latest techniques by reading books, watching instructional videos, and attending football clinics.

One very good clinic is offered by Offense-Defense Football Camps, which has clinics around the country each summer. They were voted the best football camp in America and are the official camp of the National Football League.

Relating football to other interests

Metaphors, as defined in the dictionary, are figures of speech in which one object is likened to another by speaking of it as if it were that other. Metaphors can broaden a player's imagination and link an image to an action. Metaphors help relate something you're trying to teach to something a player might understand. I use metaphors most often when I'm teaching individual skills, such as blocking and tackling. Blocking and tackling are the most important and hardest skill for young football players to learn.

For example, when I'm teaching blocking to my players, I suggest that blocking in football is like sumo wrestling. Players must wrestle their opponents away from the line of scrimmage. When I teach tackling, I suggest that players performing the skill are like cowboys at the rodeo (who must lasso the calf's legs to bring the calf down). In football terms, that means "wrap and squeeze the ball carrier's legs until they fall to the ground."

A coach can come up with metaphors for any skill on the football field. But make sure you come up with metaphors that your players will understand. Many young players are active in many sports now. You can easily ask the players for a show of hands of who is active in other sports besides football. With this feedback, you can relate your metaphors. For instance, a coach can use a baseball pitcher's throwing mechanics to teach young quarterbacks passing techniques that will allow them to throw the ball more accurately. We can also teach a defensive football player's two-point stance by relating it to a soccer goalie protecting a goal. Soccer goalies have a shoulder-width, two-point stance also. Soccer goalies are also alert, with their hands ready and positioned out in front of their bodies, ready to defend their goal. Young players who can relate to these types of images will always remember them.

Most metaphors can be funny if you think about it. It's that humor, that image, the kids will remember the next time they perform their task. Here's a funny metaphor I use when I'm teaching the concept of defense. I explain to my defensive players that the offensive line is the wall of a castle. Behind that wall are the king and queen (quarterback and runningback) who you must capture. The front defensive line's job is to push and break down the wall to cause the king and queen to flee. Whoever escapes from behind those walls will be the responsibility of linebackers to clean up and conquer.

Tutoring for kids who need help

A coach will always have players who need extra attention to hone their skills or increase their knowledge of the game. It's important to get every player on the same page so that substituting players in a game will be a smooth transition. You don't want to shuffle players who are lost or confused. By giving certain players extra attention, you may also be doing yourself a favor by developing a player for next year who will probably be a starter.

It is always difficult to give one-on-one attention to players during practices, because that takes away from the rest of the team. This is where a coaching staff can be a real benefit to you and the team. Assistant coaches can work with players in small groups by position or in individual drills.

Find time to tutor kids near the end or beginning of practice; tutoring a kid in the middle can be a distraction to other players. Breaking down into small groups is a great way to help kids maintain focus and work on technique. In full-team drills, players seem to get lethargic and are easily distracted. Small-group sessions allow coaches time to observe players' strengths and weakness and give players the tools to get better.

Announce often to your team that one-on-one time is open to players who want to improve at a skill. Shy at first, eventually players always seem to get comfortable enough to ask a coach for help in all sorts of football skills.

Budgeting for practice equipment

In my opinion, you don't have to go out and buy expensive blocking sleds and dummies to make your practices effective. Blocking sleds and dummies can be good for giving kids a break from beating on each other during practice, but sleds are very hard to move at the youth level—which means that they can defeat their own purpose. Blocking sleds are used to perfect offense players' form by teaching them to drive defensive players backward. Once young players see that the sled is not moving, however, they will adjust, lose form, and use any means possible to move the sled, which is not the correct way to teach blocking.

I have always liked game-assimilation drills where kids can work out with each other. A blocking sled is not going to spin, slap, or hold; it won't be agile, like a live person. Sleds are good as a substitute once in a while, but do not depend on them as your only instrument for teaching blocking.

If you're interested, there are inexpensive ways to purchase a blocking sled or dummies. One way is to go to your local high school or college to see if they will donate any of their older equipment. Usually schools upgrade their equipment from year to year. I would also try putting an ad in the newspaper, asking if anyone would like to donate equipment they may have stowed away over the years.

Purchasing new practice equipment will cost you anywhere from eighty-five dollars for a dummy to a couple of thousand dollars for a blocking sled. Season fund-raisers can raise some money by selling T-shirts, mugs, and raffle tickets.

Whatever you decide on, make sure you have a place to store your equipment so that nothing is vandalized or stolen.

Props and teaching aids

Any prop or teaching technique will be helpful in teaching kids football. Blocking dummies and sleds are good for demonstrating the basics and fundamentals. Children seem to learn most efficiently with visual demonstrations. That is why it's a good idea to have a drawing board around or even have a videotape session once a week to go over technique and fundamentals.

Erasable marker boards are like blackboards, but are much quicker to write on and less messy. An array of marker colors can differentiate drawings from one another. This marker board can be handy in giving your players a bird's-eye view of the Xs and Os of football. Coaches can diagram all the positions on the field and explain their duties. A coach can draw detailed strategies of how offensive players can block a desired running lane on offense or teach defensive players what direction to slant to clog a gap on defense. A marker board is often most helpful just before the team executes plays. The team can see the play, visualize how it is supposed to work, and then execute it on the practice field. Players can also ask questions—and even add some suggestions on how the play can work better.

The board can also help a coach keep a tight practice schedule by listing a timeline of things to do for that particular practice session. A timeline will have your practice sessions running more smoothly and at a quickened pace. Place the board close to the practice field as if it were a billboard. This way all the players can see what is expected of them when they get to the practice field that day.

Seven

Playing with Fear

Fear can be a major hindrance to a young player's performance. It could be the fear of physically getting hurt. It can be the mental aspect of not absorbing the game as fast as the other kids. The greatest way to deal with fear in football is experience. Over time young football players will shed the fearful beliefs they had about football. They will learn to relax, and concentrate on the team objective at hand.

Fear of contact

Physical contact will be the most fearful experience a young football player will have in football. In football, contact cannot be avoided. It's part of the game. By reading a young player's body language, a coach can tell who needs some extra encouragement and extra help. Always start shy or beginner players in close-contact hitting drills (blocking or tackling). Through repetition young players will get more comfortable with contact. Once players realize it's hard to get hurt with the protective equipment on, they will begin to break out of their shell. Players will just have to recognize that collisions are part of the game and will have to put their fears to rest.

Fear, a lot of the time, is the cause of so many injuries. The thought of fear naturally stresses a human being's nervous system and ultimately tenses the muscles, which does not allow the body to be limber to absorb collisions. A football player must be relaxed, so the muscles and tendons can stretch freely with the rigors of the game.

Sometimes what kids expect is what they will get. If a young player is focused on getting hurt, then guess what? He probably will! Even a nick or scratch is a big deal to young kids, because they are focused on the pain of the injury. It's a coach's job to identify players who are timid about contact. These players must be taught slowly to accept contact.

One of benefits of starting football early is the gradual increase in contact. From the youth level to high school, the intensity of the hits will increase. After having been hit so many times, the athlete will be used to contact. The adrenaline rush from all the action will overwhelm the thought of fear. Young players will learn to relax and absorb contact, rather than being jolted by hits and losing focus on their responsibilities.

Fear of misunderstanding

Some kids will be afraid of misunderstanding the responsibilities of their position, either because they haven't been paying attention, or because they are self-conscious about their ability to succeed. Sometimes coaches just do not have enough time to work on individual skills in practice. Most positions require a great amount of detailed instruction and can be complicated for young kids. This is why it's important for kids to pay attention in practice; their knowledge will quell fears of mistakes.

It's a good idea to write a playbook for offense and defense teams. This way kids won't have the excuse of not knowing where to be on the field. A playbook diagrams formations and schemes the team will execute throughout the season. Do not make the mistake of adding complicated plays from your old high-school or college playbook. You can, however, pick some basic and simple plays your players will be able to execute. Straight-on blocking is recommended when designing plays. Then you can later adjust the blocking assignments to different defenses you may be facing.

Knowledge is power. It's much easier to coach players who have gained some knowledge of the game by studying their playbook. I always find myself playing the more knowledgeable players over the athletic players, because they just seem to execute better and have a feel for the game.

The pecking order

I observed early on in my coaching career that children often carry a **complex** about themselves that holds them back from being productive players. Children evaluate themselves by comparing their skills to their peers. When children initially achieve poor results in an activity, they begin to believe that they simply aren't good at it; they settle for being ordinary and just fitting in. They put their productive teammates on pedestals while placing themselves in the middle or at the bottom of the pecking order. Some kids are just happy being on the team and wearing the team jersey to school.

It takes a lot of perseverance to encourage your players to become a lot more than just practice dummies. With practice and experience, these down-on-their-luck kids can gain confidence in their skills. Coaches can be their players' biggest fans. Praise the good things they do, and don't make a big fuss when they do poorly. Encouragement is the most important block for building success. Play after play, football players will gain confidence in their abilities. Along the way, kids will gain positive feedback from their peers, families, and coaches. It's this positive feedback that encourages kids to be more than just a number at the bottom of the pecking order.

Learning to channel emotions

What makes a great professional athlete is the ability to switch on the focused intensity and play aggressively during practice or in a game. Professional athletes in general live very normal, everyday lives, but when they arrive on the athletic field, they are able to suddenly increase their intensity, like Jekyll becoming Hyde, and let out all their aggressiveness on the field. This channel of emotion can be a great outlet; it allows kids to release their stress from their daily lives. But once a player is off the field, they need to socialize in an appropriate manner, as professionals do. Football at any level is an aggressive sport. If a football player does not match the intensity of his or her opponents, he or she will undoubtedly become a punching bag for the opposition. It's not easy to motivate young players to be aggressive. Kids have to challenge themselves and switch on the intensity that will allow them to compete with others. Some kids have a natural ability to compete. Other players will get pushed around for a while, and then all of a sudden realize they can take no more. I always tell my players, "It is more hurtful do nothing than it is to take action."

After the end of each week of practice, I tell my players to watch a good football movie. I want them to get inspired. I want them to have passion for this game they are playing. Some great movies to watch are *Rudy*, *Invincible*, *Little Giants*, and *The Waterboy*.

Pumping up the troops

Football is more mentally challenging than physically challenging for a player. The self-challenge of remembering plays, using techniques, and preparing yourself for some hitting is mentally taxing for any player, let alone a youngster. All eleven players on the field have to play their position well if the team is going to execute plays as a unit. Mental lapses can be more damaging to a team than physical injuries; strategic offensive and defensive schemes can be blown, and penalties can mount.

Here's a good drill to get kids mentally and physically prepared to play. This drill will have your players visualize their performance in a practice session or game. Have your players sit in a circle. Next, have your players close their eyes and imagine themselves in an upcoming game. With their eyes closed, have the kids describe how they would emotionally and physically feel if they made a great tackle or a block in a game. Would they feel strong, and maybe stand a little taller? Would they high-five and bang helmets with their teammates? Would they strut around with confidence?

If you can get your kids to visualize their success clearly enough, they may actually feel the adrenaline flowing through their bodies as if they were really in a game. They can feel it, breathe it, and live the experience as if it's really happened. This is a great way to get players thinking positively as they get ready for an upcoming game.

Motivating players

You will learn that you constantly need to give motivational speeches. Kids need a pick-me-up from time to time. They are tired from schoolwork; they get easily distracted by others. I usually have to give a short speech once a week to motivate kids to keep working hard and giving all-out effort. If you can enlighten a child, they will have a new perspective on topics they already understood. For instance, I sometimes motivate players by telling them that football is entertainment. That means people watching a football game want to be entertained by the execution, organization, and discipline of the game. Football fans do not want to see sloppy play, disorganization, and lack of effort. You have to be a special athlete to play football at any level. That is why football is popular on television: Fans want to be entertained by football players at whatever position they play. Fans want to see great catches, runs, passes, blocks, and tackles. Football players have to rehearse during the week, just as actors do for a play or a television sitcom.

Speeches like these put football in perspective for young football players. You have to remember all kids love attention. If they know they are putting on a show, they will get their act together. If young children can think of themselves as entertainers, it will give them a feeling of importance.

Eight

Three Keys to a Winning Football Program

There are three keys to building a winning football program at the youth level:

- Players must be well-conditioned.
- Players must have well-developed blocking skills.
- Players must have well-developed tackling skills.

These three keys allow your team to play well consistently for long periods of time that will physically wear down the opposing teams.

Physical conditioning allows athletes, even young ones, to put out 100 percent effort on every play. Well-conditioned athletes are stronger, faster, and more focused. Conditioned athletes can physically wear down their opponents, causing the opponent to let up on plays and eventually quit.

Usually teams cannot deliver a consistent intensity level, play in and play out, if they are not conditioned properly. When an opposing team cannot match your team's work ethic on each play, it's to your advantage. Many coachess do not take conditioning seriously. Many people think football uses energy in short spurts, where players can catch their breath between plays. This is nonsense. Play after play, kids are getting physically fatigued from blocking, tackling, and chasing the other team around.

Conditioning also gives your team a psychological advantage. Your players' relentless tempo will have the opposing players wondering, "Are we ever going to get a breather?" Offensively you will have the advantage needed to drive the ball down the field at will. On defense, your team will have the energy to stop the opposing team in their tracks. Football is not all about size and muscles. It's about brains, strategy, and a good work ethic.

The arena of blocking and tackling is the most technical, and the least liked by young football players. If a young player can learn to block and tackle, then he or she can play any position on the football field. Blocking and tackling are also the most dangerous skills if a football player has poor technical form. A coach's first concern for his or her young football players is safety. Poor blocking and tackling technique can cause neck and spinal cord injuries, the most serious injuries a football player can face.

This chapter will go into great detail on how to get kids interested in blocking and tackling as challenging but safe skills. You can never do too many block-and-tackle drills in practice. These are the two chores that allow you to move the ball offensively down the field and to defensively stop the opposing team.

Conditioning

Stretching

A stretching regimen will benefit your football program in many ways. Stretching before every practice and game is the first structured formation your players will learn. Teach your team to be disciplined enough to get in straight lines and rows before every practice, with an equal amount of space between each player to allow comfortable stretching. Remember that organization reflects the coach's control over the team.

Stretching sessions can be an important time for players to spiritually prepare themselves for the day's work. It's always a good ritual to have your players stretch in a yoga fashion, so they can get in touch with their emotions and body. Football has a lot to do with focus. Focusing on the play assignments and techniques will help players by giving them the confidence to perform to their very best capability.

Stretching can be a football player's best asset. Stretching offers the benefit of improved range of motion in joints and ligaments, which will prevent sprains and pulls. Increasing the range of motion throughout a football player's body can improve coordination, strength, and speed—and prevent injury. For instance, flexibility of the upper body—shoulders, chest, and back—can improve pushing power for blocking on the offensive side of the ball. On the defensive side, players will have the range of motion to wrap their arms around the ball carrier's legs and make a perfect tackle.

Be creative in picking stretching positions that are beneficial to football players. Do the same sequence of stretches at each practice, so the routine will become familiar. A stretching program should last twenty minutes, with a warm-up before and after, to get the blood flowing in any tensed muscles that remain in your young athletes.

Stretching

Hurler Stretch   Standing Toe Touch

Split Legged Toe Touch

Push-up Back Stretch

Plyometrics

Jump Squats   Power Jumping Jacks

One-legged Hops   Explosive Push-ups

Plyometric exercises

Plyometrics is a popular training technique used by strength trainers to improve an athlete's overall performance in coordination, strength, and muscle endurance. Plyometric exercises are natural calisthenic movements that require spurts of explosive effort to get maximum benefit. Plyometric exercises include hopping, bounding, jumping, lunging, squatting, and skipping—exercises that involve a variety of muscles, tendons, and ligaments that are rarely used. Plyometrics is a perfect exercise program for children and teens who want to begin strength training. Kids naturally love to jump, hop, skip, bound, and be active in something new and challenging.

Over the years, plyometrics have been used to correct imbalances in coordination and strength. For example, most athletes have a dominant arm or leg that they depend on to give them power. Plyometric training adds an equal amount of stress to the weaker muscles, which will eventually strengthen and meet the same standards as the dominant muscles, creating a balance of strength throughout the body.

Here are some guidelines to follow when leading your players through plyometric training. Jumps should always begin at ground level and be closely supervised. Keep away from advanced stages of plyometrics that call for depth jumping and drop jumping, which involve jumps from boxes or benches. Make sure that only body weight is being used when performing a set. Give an athlete an adequate amount of rest between sets of exercise. Choose five to seven exercises per workout, to be repeated for two to three sets. For example, one daily workout could include high knees, walking lunges, one-legged hops, bounding, and power skips.

Plyometrics can also be an excellent warm-up activity to get your players ready for practice or games. A series of hops, jumps, and skips will fire the muscle fibers and warm up the tendons of your young athletes. Soon after stretching is completed, have the team execute some plyometrics.

Learning while conditioning

The first three weeks of practice should involve lots of conditioning work, supplemented with basics and fundamentals of the game. Kill two birds with one stone by working your offensive and defensive systems in while the kids are conditioning.

For instance, have eleven players line up in an offensive formation, like the wishbone formation, and do sprints down the field. Defensively, you can have eleven players aligned in a 4–4 defense and do back peddling work. By having players do conditioning work in offensive formations and defensive alignments, you give your players familiarity with where they are supposed to be positioned on the football field. If this is not practiced early in your preseason, your kids will be absolutely lost on the football field. This strategy will also help you as a coach in the long run. When you call out an offensive formation, all the players on the roster will know what you're talking about. Defensively, you can call out a defensive alignment, like a 5–3 defense, and all your players will assume their positions.

Young football players have to feel comfortable on the football field. A big part of that is the knowledge of where to be positioned on the field. It's a very good idea to do these drills right from the first day of practice. It will make your job teaching offensive and defensive football down the road much easier.

Creative conditioning drills

Any type of continuous running will condition your players' heart and lungs. This will benefit them in practice and in games. Jogging laps around the football field is a great example of an endurance-building exercise. The body's lungs will learn to expand to gather more air. The loss of body fat will put less strain on the heart. Short-spurt exercises are effective only if there is minimal rest in between.

Most children are not enthused about exercising, especially running. As a matter of fact, they dread it. It's boring and hard, and it's not fun to be grabbing your ribs when you're finished. Be creative in coming up with endurance exercises that distract players from their hardships. In other words, make a game out of exercise, shifting attention to the challenge of the game, not the conditioning aspect. Your players won't even realize they are getting in shape. Below are some good activities that will accomplish this. Add a football to any game for added development of motor skills related to football.

The **circuit** can be done in a square area fifteen yards long on each side (marked with cones). Start the drill in a three-point stance. For the first fifteen yards, the players will **carioca** (move in crossover steps). For the second fifteen yards, the players will **crabwalk** (move on all fours). For the third fifteen yards the players will run backward, and for the last fifteen yards, the players will sprint. If you drop a ball in a player's area, he or she can practice recovering fumbles.

The **offensive hurry-up drill** is another good conditioning drill. Set up a seven-man offensive line with one quarterback behind. Set up another seven-man line and quarterback side by side. On each quarterback's cadence (snap count), both teams will sprint ten yards and immediately get into a three-point stance. Drive down the hundred-yard field in spurts of ten yards. Keep driving down the field in a hurry-up fashion. Set teams back five yards if they go off sides.

Relay races are a fun drill that kids will enjoy. Split players into two equal lines (Team A and Team B). Have two cones set up in front of each team and two more cones set up twenty yards down field. The first player in line for each team will have a football in hand. The drill will start on the coach's cadence. The first player from each line will release, run twenty yards down and around the cone, and sprint back to relay the football to the next teammate in line. The next two players in line will release and do the same until everyone on Team A and Team B has gone.

This drill is good for ending your practice. It's also great ball-handling drill to help kids learn to tuck the ball away during an all-out sprint.

Indian runs put a twist on running. Start the team in one single-file line. Place your heaviest kids toward the front of the line. The drill will start with a slow jogging pace. The last player in line must sprint to the front of the line, then continue the slow jogging pace. Then the next player at the end of the line will sprint to the front and continue the pace. Keep this rotation going until everyone has gone once.

Training on hills is great conditioning for an athlete. Hills can build stamina, balance, coordination, and leg strength. Hill training can break the monotony of the same old routine. Hill training is something different and may stimulate more interest in practice. Be creative in doing drills on a hill. You can do a series of sprinting, crabbing, and back-peddling drills up and down the hill. Add a ball for added difficulty and concentration. I have also had my offensive team run plays up a hill, then jog back down for another sequence. You can even get adventurous by having your defense do tackling drills on a hill.

A healthy coach

Youth football coaches can harbor a lot of stress, and aggravated nerves can prompt them to pick up bad habits to release these stresses. Coaches may become more moody, eat improperly, smoke, drink, and lack the motivation to be productive.

Exercise can be your greatest asset by far. It's another advantage to coaching youth athletics: seeing the players conditioning during the week will inspire you to do your own fitness program. People tend to eat more nutritiously when they are on an exercise program. Exercise also tends to help people to feel better about themselves, which can contribute to stress relief. Fitness activities can help a coach be more creative; the release of stress through exercise can help a coach think more clearly about designing new plays and preparation techniques for football. Being in shape will also help a coach lead practices more constructively. A fit coach can demonstrate plays and conditioning drills to young players.

Over time, coaches can condition themselves to relax. Lifestyle adjustments such as getting adequate sleep and exercise, eating more healthfully, being more organized, and thinking things through before reacting will reduce stress. On your days off, find activities that will put your nerves at ease: going fishing, reading a book, or enjoying the ballgame on television. Make time for yourself to avoid the burnout that could result from the abundance of work you do.

Reducing stress will do a great deal of good for you and everyone around you. You'll think much more clearly and make better decisions. Wouldn't it be nice to not only give your players a great experience in football, but to also give yourself the gift of a longer, healthier, stress-free life?

Conditioning conclusion

Never push your players over the limit. Children are at greater risk of becoming dehydrated than adults because of their lighter body weight and higher turnover of water. Tell your players to drink lots of water throughout the day. Dehydration has to be taken very seriously in youth football. Practices begin in the late summer months, and young players have the task of competing with protective equipment on. Teach players the warning signs of dehydration: dry mouth, dizziness, confusion, rapid heart rate, and lethargy. Coaches should always be aware of how hard they are pushing their players. Frequent water breaks can keep your players energized, as well as give you a moment to organize for the next objective on your day's agenda. Be sure to ease your players into your conditioning program.

Conditioning can be very beneficial to coaches in several ways. They will feel better about themselves. They will move from drill to drill at a more upbeat pace. Players will become more unified as a team. Your players will play at a higher athletic level than most opposing teams. Last but not least, conditioning sessions at practice will weed out the players who are not really interested in playing football or who are not taking it seriously. These are the players who will eventually quit. The ones who do stick around are usually the ones who have passion for the game of football.

Block and tackle

Organized football is all about **full contact**. The essence of the game is blocking and tackling. Blocking and tackling should be taught early and often in your practices. The best time to start is the first week of camp, with no pads on. This may seem out of the norm, but this method will allow players to focus on the basics of football with no distractions. The sights and sounds of plastic equipment crashing throughout practice is intimidating to young players, especially first-time players.

Players will also be able to move freely without the distracting friction of the tight uniforms snug against their little bodies. Equipment-free practice allows players to focus freely on technical footwork and hand-to-hand combat skills used in blocking and tackling.

All drills should be closely supervised and done in close quarters, at a walk-through pace or half speed.

Offensive blocking skills

What makes football the ultimate team sport is that all eleven players on the field have to work simultaneously at their positions to be successful. This is especially true for players on the offensive team, who have to work together to make a series of strategic blocks. Blocking is the most underappreciated skill in football—and the most important to the offensive team's success in moving the ball down the field. Most kids don't value the skill of blocking, because it is not a glorified achievement. Announcers and analysts for professional football seldom call out the names of offensive linemen making a terrific block. Their names are usually mentioned when there's a penalty involved, like off sides or holding. The skill positions seem to get all the accolades on television. Kids just perceive blocking as boring. You can usually see it in their performance. Young football players just seem lazy and never hold their blocks for too long.

Your objective is to make blocking interesting and fun so kids can find some value in doing it. First off, let's not sugarcoat the manner in which a block is supposed to be executed. Football players need an aggressive and physical attitude if they are going to compete with determined defensive players. Blockers must be free of fear, and they must strategically block the opposing defender.

Begin by associating the task of blocking with a fun concept kids can identify with. Explain to your players that blocking is a shoving match between them and the defender. The object of the game is to shove or push an opponent out of position and off the line of scrimmage.

Kids can also identify with the idea that blocking is like a sumo-wrestling match; they must wrestle the opponent from their existing position and out of the circle. Young players have great imaginations. Players will learn to visualize themselves having fun wrestling (blocking) opponents out of running lanes, so ball carriers can run freely down the field.

Fear of Blocking

Another reason young football players are reluctant to block is that they are scared of the contact involved with the task. They are doubly scared of confronting aggressive defenders who they may have to block in practice or a game. The physical size and strength of some opponents just overpowers some players. It's going to be your job to slowly ease your players into blocking.

To combat the fear of blocking, a coach can match up kids of similar physical size and strength when performing full-contact blocking drills in practice. Being paired with someone their own size will give kids confidence and allow them to focus on proper form and technique, knowing they are not going to get run over by the opposition. Experiment from time to time with giving these timid players someone bigger and stronger to block, so that they can slowly build the belief in themselves that they can block anyone.

Teach your young team how important blocking is to moving the ball offensively. Explain to them that one player cannot score a touchdown alone. Football is not a game of "kill the carrier." One ball carrier, no matter how talented he or she is, cannot juke and sprint past eleven potential tacklers and score a touchdown on every play. Offensively, football is about the team, as a unit, strategically setting blocks (screens) against opposing defenses so that a ball carrier can move the ball down the field.

The three-point stance

The idea of the **three-point stance** is to give the offensive player leverage over his or her opponent. The goal is to use a low center of gravity for balance combined with a charge upward and underneath the opponent's shoulder pads to push the opponent off the line of scrimmage and away from the ball carrier.

A three-point stance should be practiced from the first day of camp. Beginning football players should also practice it at home. It will take weeks or even the entire season for some of your players to achieve a comfortable and effective three-point stance.

In a standing or **ready position**, players should have their feet spread slightly wider than shoulder width. In a **down position**, players should squat down with their head up and back straight (squat two-point stance). In the **set position**, players plant their dominant hand (fingers) into ground. There should be slight weight on the fingertips. Insufficient weight forward on the fingertips could cause a jump off sides or a lunge out of the stance. Leaning forward too much also will cause the player's head to droop down; you don't want players to lose sight of their targets. The opposite arm can rest across the opposite thigh.

The balance of the player's weight should be distributed on the ball of each foot. The dominant foot can be set back slightly (toes of back foot even with front heel). The slight offsetting of the dominant foot allows the player to spring out of his or her stance at the snap of the ball.

As a coach, you'll probably need to **troubleshoot** your players' stances. It's funny: coaches can demonstrate a solid three-point stance and still get some awful imitations from their players. The most common problems with young football players' stances are rounded backs, spider legs, and even some sprinter stances.

Here's where a coach will need some patience. You can spend hours demonstrating, and players still won't be physically comfortable in a three-point stance. Let kids practice at home. Have them use a mirror at home, so they can see themselves in a three-point stance.

Two types of blocking

There are many types of blocking techniques, but the two most basic are **run blocking** and **pass blocking**. Run blocking is as strategic as any chess move. Every defensive player is assigned to block on any given play. Football is a battle of territory. Run blocking moves the opponent from the line of scrimmage to create running lanes for the offensive ball carrier. The game of football was originally based on moving the ball methodically down the field with run blocking—and a strong-willed ball carrier to boot. The passing game came along when football became too dangerous, with players wearing insufficient equipment and getting hurt far too often. The revolution of the passing game to advance the ball down the field made pass blocking essential to protecting the quarterback.

This chapter will go into detail about teaching young kids how to run and pass block. It's important for a coach to glorify blocking and make it interesting; otherwise, some young players will associate "blocking" with "boring." In teaching the physical skill, we will use a lot of metaphors, word associations, and demonstrations to give new associations to the term "blocking."

Run blocking

Charging is the first key element in performing a block on the offensive line. Offensive linemen can charge out of their three-point stances and neutralize the opponent's forward momentum. The battle in the trenches (line of scrimmage) is usually won by the quickest offensive or defensive lineman who fires out off the ball. The players generating the most momentum forward are the most successful.

Offensive linemen can take advantage of the charge, because they know the quarterback's snap count. A quick charge at the snap of the ball can also help an offensive lineman against more aggressive and bigger defensive linemen.

The charge leads to a **forearm smash**. An offensive lineman can charge leading with his or her forearms and connecting right underneath the defender's shoulder pads. The combination of the charge and forearm smash will stand the opponent up and allow the offensive lineman to gain leverage and eventually drive the opponent backward.

At the beginning of the charge, the elbows are positioned out. Fists are clenched at chest level. Once contact is made, offensive linemen must drive their opponents back with short, choppy steps, keeping their legs wide and maintaining their balance. Extending their arms into the defender is the last step in maintaining the block. Offensive linemen can use the palms of their hands to control the defender's movements.

Golden rule to run blocking

In run blocking, it is important that blockers know which direction to push or screen their opponents away from the play. The golden rule to remember is that opponents should be blocked from anywhere the play is designed to be executed. Two techniques can stop a defender from getting to the ball carrier. In the first, an offensive blocker gets his or her helmet across the defender's torso to stop the defender's momentum. This allows the blocker's entire body to be involved. In the second, an offensive blocker uses a defensive player's own momentum to his or her advantage. The offensive blocker can simply get his or her helmet across the torso of the defensive lineman and at the same time use the opponent's momentum to push him or her past the running lane, causing the defender to over pursue the play, which will ultimately open up cut back lanes for ball carriers to run through.

Teaching with "sumo drills"

I truly believe that if you want kids to learn, they must be interested in the subject. Making a subject fun will spark kids' interest. Blocking is the most important task on offense. It's also the least appreciated by young players. This blocking drill has all the elements of good blocking technique—plus, it's fun.

I call this drill a **sumo drill**. The sport of sumo wrestling involves technical skills similar to those an offensive lineman needs in football. The mechanics involve keeping a low center of gravity and maintaining balance, leverage, upper-body strength, and leg drive. In the sumo drill, young players will learn to charge, use a forearm smash, and develop hand-to-hand combat skills to control their opponents' movements and eventually move the opponents from the line of scrimmage. To start the drill, have the entire team form a circle. Two players of equal size (big guys with big guys, little guys with little guys) will match up, facing each other in the middle of the ring. Both players should take on a low, wide, squatting sumo stance. You can later have your players practice this drill in a three-point stance. For now I want the kids getting the concept that blocking is like sumo wrestling. If they have fun with this drill, they'll start to enjoy blocking.

Start the match on the coach's cadence ("ready, sumo"). The object of the game is to push, charge, and forearm smash the opponent until the opponent is out of the ring. The first one to do so is the winner.

Supervision is a must in this game. We are working on technique here; we're not here to see who is the dominant player. When your young players start to relate sumo to football blocking, they will become more enthused about blocking.

Remember to take breaks between each match to explain to your players that a low center of gravity, balance, leverage, and leg drive are key to moving opponents, just like on the football field.

It's very important to quiz players about the drills:

- Why are we in a wide stance?

- Why are we staying low?

- Why are we driving our legs in short, choppy steps?

- What's the art of getting leverage?

Pass-blocking technique

The key to pass blocking is to mirror the movements of the defender rushing the passer. The offensive line should not charge out of their stances, as in run blocking. Rather, they should make the defender come to them, **mirroring** the defender's every move. In pass blocking, offensive linemen can use their hands to gain separation and control the defensive players' movements. A combination of quick feet and active hand-to-hand combat skills can protect offensive linemen from tactics (spin moves, bull rushes, and so on) used by defensive players to get to the ball carrier.

You can help players understand pass blocking by comparing pass blocking with playing defense in basketball. When defending the basket against a basketball carrier, a defensive player needs quick feet to deflect the player from driving to the basket for a score. The same concept goes for an offensive lineman defending against a defensive lineman. A defensive lineman's goal is to sack the quarterback. An offensive lineman must use quick feet and mirror the defender's every move in order to deflect the defender from the quarterback.

One particularly good pass-blocking drill involves having one offensive and defensive lineman face off. Place a football about seven yards behind the offensive lineman. At the sound of the whistle, the defensive lineman will try to recover the football by eluding your pass blocker. The pass blocker's job is to deflect the defensive lineman from the football, as if the football were the quarterback.

This drill will challenge a pass blocker's **mechanics** in footwork and upper-body strength. If the pass blocker is beaten by the defensive player, have them go to the end of the line until you can find a pass blocker who is consistent and up to the challenge. Once you find a consistent pass blocker, compliment them and challenge the rest of the team to mimic the consistent player's actions in protecting the football.

Once the team gets the hang of it, you can then try a 7–7 match up. In a 7–7 match up, you'll have a full offensive and defensive line butting heads. This time, place the football ten yards behind the offensive center. In this game, every pass blocker who gets beaten by a defensive lineman is eliminated from the game and replaced by another pass blocker, until there is only one pass blocker left—the most consistent of the bunch.

Playbook for linemen

We always want to make blocking exciting. Kids need to see blocking as an important assignment—especially young offensive linemen. Always keep the concept of blocking fresh and interesting. It's a good idea to design blocking schemes, so your players can get involved in the game plan and also have some fun. Offensive linemen love to get outside and run, so design some pulling plays (sweep outside to block) in which your linemen can make blocks downfield. Pull your offensive tackles on inside plays.

You can also draw up some one-on-one blocking schemes, double-team schemes, or triple-team schemes. Give your blocking schemes some catchy or goofy names that your kids will enjoy using when a play calls for it. My personal favorite is a "roadkill block." This blocking scheme calls for the center and the two guards to triple-team the nose tackle (who is lined up over the offensive center) for a quick-run play up the middle. You can even specialize some plays using a lineman's name. This will really give the player a sense of worth and attention.

Mistakes young linemen make

Blocking takes a lot of skill, technique, balance, leverage, strength, and coordination. This is why your practices need to focus on it so much. All your players should learn how to block. The more players who know how to block, the stronger your team will be offensively. If kids like the contact of blocking, then they'll like the contact of tackling on defense, which will make your entire team stronger. Below are some mistakes to look out for when your offensive team is blocking:

- Off sides: player leans or gets distracted.
- Lunging: player uses poor stance, is out of control.
- Missed blocks: player is slow, out of stance, intimidated, with head down.
- Poor stance: player's head is down, with back bowed and legs straight.

- Failure to sustain blocks: blockers do not drive their legs or extend arms into the opponent.

- Holding: player grabs a jersey or hooks a defender's arm.

Motivation for team blocking

Kids have to be motivated to block as a team. I'll go back to the metaphor I used earlier, but this time for the offensive line. This is such a great metaphor that kids grasp, because they can relate to fairy tale books their parents may have read them growing up as a child. I always explain to my teams that the offensive line is a castle wall, and the backfield players are soldiers to protect the crown of the king and queen. "Castles were built to keep enemies from conquering the king and queen's treasures. Enemies would try to tear them down the walls, or do anything in their means to get behind them. Football on the offensive side of the ball is the same concept. You are the walls protecting the royal football from being captured. Defenders will try every defensive strategy to get the ball. You must be prepared and work as a team. There can be no cracks in the wall. Everyone should have the same goal: to keep the wall strong."

Offensive philosophy at the youth level

Here's some great advice, especially for a first-year head coach: When drawing a game plan for opposing teams, make sure you attack the center of the opposing defense. Make it the focal point of your offense. Run right between your two guards and center. This will be the **core** of your offense.

A few circumstances are behind this concept. First, the shortest distance from point A to point B is a straight line. Second, young opposing defensive players do not like to make head-on tackles when a ball carrier has a full head of steam. If you run the ball up the middle from time to time, your chances of breaking a big gainer go up dramatically. Third, you will always have a shortage of good, solid blockers on your team. So put your best three at the center and two guard positions.

Teach some good one-on-one blocking schemes to your linemen early in the season. Be sure to teach the guards to release and get the middle linebackers. Finally, find a tough, fearless, and explosive ball carrier (fullback) to run up that middle. Disguise your main play (fullback dive up the middle) with some clever misdirection, motion, and ball fakes. You can also use a variety of offensive formations such as a wing-T, I formation, wishbone, and power I formation to confuse the defensive team even more.

Once you establish the run up the middle, everything else opens up. But always go back to the bread-and-butter play to keep teams honest. Keep pounding, and soon you'll break a big one. I've been in many rainy or snowy games where we had no choice but to run up the middle, because there was no traction. That's how football was originally meant to be played, with solid blocking and aggressive running of the ball.

Defensive tackling skills

What is tackling? Tackling involves the eleven players on the defensive side of the ball trying to wrestle the opposing team's ball carrier to the ground. The defensive unit has the common goal of stopping the offensive team from getting the ball into the end zone for a score. Defense is inherent in the philosophy of tackling the opposing ball carrier.

In reality, defensive players must try to predict the opposing team's plays, place themselves in the right position, shed blockers, and ultimately make a tackle on the ball carrier. By far the most significant attribute of a defensive player is tackling ability. Tackling is an art. It needs to be practiced more often than any other defensive tactic on defense.

Ninety percent of performing a tackle is desire. Football players must have the will to make a tackle. It sounds easy, but there is an approach and an attitude that defensive players need to have. Potential tacklers must be in the right place, in the right position, and use the proper technique to stop the ball carrier.

Technique will be paramount to safely teaching young football players how to tackle successfully. Most football injuries occur due to poor tackling form. Many young players lead with their heads down, which leaves them prone to serious neck injuries. In this chapter we will review some innovative techniques that give young football players the motivation to tackle successfully.

Fear of tackling

Just as with blocks, a young football player can be hindered by the fear of contact. Young players may fear the jolt or the physical pain that can occur during a tackle.

Kids are aware that the more steam a ball carrier builds up, the harder the collision will be. The only way to stop that kind of force is to match that force with your own head of steam. Football players need this aggressive confidence in themselves if they are going to even attempt to tackle. You can teach all the basics and fundamentals you want, but you will always have at least one young player who shies away from contact. Fear takes over in these young players' minds—especially beginners. Some young players feel overwhelmed by the collisions, or even by the sight of an aggressive ball carrier coming their way.

This is when a coach has to be a good motivator. It's always good idea to explain to your team that it's natural to be scared. It's also a good idea to explain the following: "What you focus on is what you'll get. If you think about getting hurt, then there's a good chance you will, because you're in a state of mind where anything related to contact is going to be painful. The mind and the nervous system work together. When the mind senses pain, the muscles seem to tense as a defense mechanism. This paralysis doesn't allow your body to relax and absorb a blow. Instead, every hit, jolt, and collision is going to be painful."

Probably the number-one tip you can give your team is to be the aggressor: "Be the hitter, not the hittee." I tell young players to think of the rewards of making a great tackle. They'll receive attention from peers, coaches, and family; all will see how brave they are in their commitment to tackling. When football players see that the benefits outweigh the cost, they lose their fear. Begin building confidence in your young tacklers by going over the basics of tackling. Use slow walkthrough drills, so kids can get their feet wet in a controlled manner.

Equipment as protection

To dampen the fear in your young players, explain the equipment that they are wearing. As you go over each piece, explain that it's all light plastic and foam. Acknowledging the equipment piece by piece will help young players not to fear the crashing sounds or potential harm.

Football equipment was made for protection. Football equipment is made to cushion and bounce to protect players. For instance, shoulder pads are like shock absorbers; they bounce on contact. This is partly why we don't want kids tackling high on a ball carrier, because the potential tackler will bounce off. Teach kids to tackle the cushioned area of a ball carrier—that is, the hips and thighs. "Cushion" is the word to use for young timid tacklers.

Tackling like a cowboy

A good metaphor for teaching kids how to tackle is to tell them to tackle (rope) like a cowboy.

First, explain to your team that tackling is like calf roping at a rodeo. In other words, players are cowboys, their arms are the lassos, and the ball carriers' legs are like those of a calf. Once cowboys lasso the calf around legs, they pull the rope tight to instantly squeeze the calf's legs, until the calf falls to the ground. Tackling involves the same concept: getting the tackler's arms around the ball carrier's legs and squeezing the legs together until the ball carrier falls to the ground.

The worst tackling form is when a player tackles too high on a ball carrier, up toward the shoulder pads. Poor form like this only allows a tackler's upper body (mainly the arms) to be involved in the tackle. The correct area to tackle is at the hip and midtorso, a region that allows the tackler's entire body to be involved, resulting in a perfect takedown.

Teach your kids to be cowboys, and I'm sure they'll make the connection.

The basics of tackling

Below are the five steps to performing a textbook tackle. We will also break down the types of tackles kids face in a game and list some drills that will prepare players for the art of tackling.

1. Start in a breakdown (ready) position. That's a half-squat two-point stance, with hands out in front of body.

2. Get square with the ball carrier. Eye the ball carrier's waistline and come up under control.

3. On angled tackles, cross the ball carrier's torso with your helmet to stop progress. For straight-on tackles, put your helmet on either side of the ball carrier.

4. Embed your shoulders into the ball carrier's hip or midtorso region.

5. Clamp your arms and hands around the ball carrier's legs, then lift while simultaneously pulling the legs together ... until the ball carrier falls to the ground!

Tackling Form

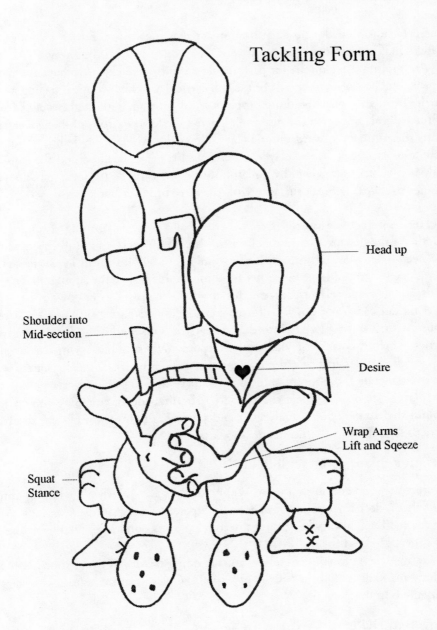

Head up

Shoulder into
Mid-section

Desire

Wrap Arms
Lift and Sqeeze

Squat
Stance

Types of tackles

Side tackles are probably the easiest tackles for young defenders to make, because the tackler doesn't have to bear the full brunt of a ball carrier coming directly at them. Head-on tackles produce the impact that most often rattles a youngster. Players may even shy away the next time a ball carrier comes their way.

An important technique for performing a solid side tackle is to have the tackler's helmet on the **correct side** of the ball carrier. A tackler who is engaging a ball carrier from an angle should use proper form of leading, with the helmet in front of the ball carrier's torso at waist level. Placing the head in front of the ball carrier stops the runner's forward progress and allows the tackler's whole body to contribute to the tackle. If the player were to put his or her head behind the runner, only the tackler's arms could wrap around the ball carrier's leg (arm tackle). The runner could easily break this grip with the force of his or her legs.

Head-on tackles usually occur when a ball carrier is running through the middle of the defense. When a ball carrier is coming head-on at full speed, tacklers need to stay low on impact. If they don't, they will learn this lesson the hard way. A tackler should put his or her head to the side, lower the shoulder into the midsection, wrap the arms, squeeze, lift, and take the ball carrier down.

A tackler can bring down ball carriers more effectively by building up speed (momentum) and exploding into the ball carrier. This kind of force jolts the ball carrier, which can cause the ball carrier to potentially stumble, giving the advantage to the tackler to bring the ball carrier to the ground. Smaller tacklers will have to generate more momentum upon impact to bring down larger ball carriers. Players should complete the tackle by simultaneously wrapping their arms around the runner's legs (thigh area) and squeezing tightly and closing the ball carrier's legs. This will result in a textbook tackle.

Designing your own tackling drills

Be creative when coming up with tackling drills. I have always liked developing drills that reflect what players will actually experience in a game. Never let a drill run for too long; always keep things fresh, so players don't lose interest or forget the concept behind the drill.

Always explain to your team why you are doing the drill. Give demonstrations of how the skill is supposed to be performed. Get the entire team involved, so everyone is in on the action.

Suggested Drills

Here are some drills that I made up myself during my years of coaching. These are great techniques for players who are just learning to tackle, and great for veteran players who want a challenge.

The **prop-tackling drill** teaches the basics of tackling: staying low, getting the head on the appropriate side of the ball carrier, wrapping the arms, and squeezing the legs together.

Begin this drill by having two players face each other. One of the players will be the ball carrier. His or her job is only to be a standing prop. The ball carrier will pretend to be running either right, left, or straight ahead, with the football in his or her outside hand. The tackler will lie on his or her back, at the feet of the prop ball carrier. On the coach's whistle, the tackler lying on the ground will turn over and perform a tackle on the prop ball barrier. Remember, teach tacklers to stay low, get their heads on the correct side of the ball carrier (head up), and finish by exploding and wrapping the ball carrier to the ground.

Practice tackling to the right, left, and straight on. Have your prop ball carriers turn in either direction as if they were running in that direction.

The **tackling on hills** drill teaches young kids how to tackle low on a ball carrier. Find a pretty steep hill around your practice area. Put a ball carrier on top of the hill, and put a tackler at the bottom of the hill. On the coach's whistle, the two players will meet in an open-field tackling situation. The benefit for the tackler is that the legs of the ball carrier are at eye level because of the incline of the hill. Have the ball carrier juke the tackler, not sprint by him at full speed. Have your tackler attack the hill and wrap the ball carrier down to the ground.

In practice, I always liked to assimilate game situations for my players. Defensively there will be many obstacles before a defensive tackler can get a clear shot at a ball carrier. The biggest obstacles are blockers. I always tell my defensive players that they are assigned to be blocked on any given play. A defensive player must be ready, aware, and alert to his or her surroundings.

In the **shedding blockers** drill, your defensive team will learn to get physical and shed oncoming blockers. This drill is an obstacle course of blockers; it's great for defensive linemen, linebackers, and players holding secondary positions.

The drill starts with three offensive blockers in a single-file line about five to seven yards apart. Behind the last blocker will be a ball carrier, who is ten yards back and is only "live" until the tackler sheds all three blockers.

Your first defensive player in line will have to fight off the first blocker, while the other blockers "freeze." After—or if—that first player sheds the first blocker, he or she moves on to the second, who becomes live, and so on, to the third blocker. Once he or she has passed the third blocker, the defensive player gets into a one-on-one, open-field tackle situation with the live ball carrier.

Blocker-shedding technique is multifaceted. Defensive players need an arsenal of skills to get past an offensive blocker. Defensive players need speed, leverage, and strength to elude blockers and get to a ball carrier or quarterback dropping back for a pass. Here are some techniques that a defensive player can use at the line of scrimmage:

- **Bull rush**: Just as in the charge in a blocking technique, a defensive lineman must stay low and drive upward underneath the blocker's shoulder pads, causing the blocker to lose balance and begin back peddling.

- **Swim technique**: One way to use a swim technique is to hook the offensive blocker's arm in attempt to knock him off balance. A second way is to extend the defensive player's arm over the offensive blocker, as if swimming over the top of the blocker. Once over the top, the defender can push off with the other arm to get past the blocker.

- **Spin technique**: The defensive player can lean into the blocker with one shoulder and use his or her momentum to spin a full 360 degrees, making his or her way around the blocker.

The **full defense tackling** drill is physical and assimilates a game environment. It tests a player's ability to make correct tackles. It also tests a tackler's endurance for making multiple consecutive tackles without losing tackling form. The drill also prepares tacklers to be alert at all times.

Begin by setting eleven defensive players in the defensive alignment of your choice. Choose a defense that you are going to use frequently throughout the season (5–3, 3–4, or 4–4 alignment, for example). On the offensive side of the ball, players will form one single-file line of ball carriers, seven yards behind the imaginary line of scrimmage.

Hand the ball off to the first ball carrier in line on the offensive side. The ball carrier will then run at a potential tackler, whom the coach will name aloud. For example, the coach could hand the ball off and say "Jon, you're live." This would mean that Jon, playing the cornerback position, will be active and will have to attempt to tackle the ball carrier. The other ten defensive players will freeze unless their named is called.

In the advanced stages, you can add a lead blocker in front of the ball carrier. You can also have a tackler make repeated tackles, one after another, by repeatedly calling that player's name. Repeated tackles build muscle endurance and prepares players to get up and be in a ready position again. You can also send two or three tacklers at a time to make a tackle on a ball carrier.

Take note of who is making tackles and who is having difficultly. If players are missing a lot of tackles, don't lash out at them. Instead have them compose themselves. Review their mistakes with them. Let them watch the other players make tackles, which might inspire them. Believe me, your tacklers will get better as a direct result of this drill. They will learn to stay low and wrap. Players do not want to embarrass themselves in front of their teammates; they will make the conscious decision to make better tackles.

Defensive philosophy at the youth level

Defense wins games. Defense can tighten up the score, even when you don't have a talented team. On defense, a coach can move players to different positions to see where they fit best. Defense can also allow coaches to get all their players in the game.

I think it is very important for a coach to have defensive schemes and play calls; this way the team can play as a unit. Defensively, schemes give a coach an advantage at the youth level. At this age, offense teams practice basic and simple blocking assignments. Defensively, you can take advantage of that by calling some line stunts (defensive linemen cross each other) or shifting the defense line. This will cause confusion on the opposing offensive line regarding whom to block.

Drawing up defensive schemes can also help you compensate for players who are not the greatest of tacklers. Change up defenses from time to time to give opposing offenses different looks. Have the offense on high alert at all times. Don't be scared to move some quick and fast guys onto the front line to change the pace. Then throw in some heavy hitters.

Through my experiences coaching football at the youth level, I have observed that the most important position on defense was the defensive end—not the linebacker, as you might assume. At the youth level, football teams love to take their fastest player and sweep them up the sideline to get an easy touchdown. To negate this strategy, I learned to position my tallest, most athletic players as defensive bookends. Tall, athletic defensive ends have a knack for chasing down quarterbacks and running backs who dart to the outside for potential big yardage gains.

In summary, by drawing up some creative defensive plays, you put your team at a great advantage. Brains, not brawn, can win games, and that's a great lesson for your team to learn.

Nine

Game Day

The day before every game, make sure you ask all your players if they will be able to make the game the next day. Knowing beforehand that some players have commitments will save you the stress of rearranging your depth chart on game day. Believe me, kids have very busy lives. Often players and parents will have prior commitments to birthday parties or vacations—or even a trip to a pro game. A coach should never coerce a player into missing a non-football event that is already planned, no matter how important the game is. Kids can make their own decisions and find out afterward if the decision was right.

The limited reliability of such young players makes it important for a coach to have substitute players who can fill in right away. Give all your second- and third-string players the experience of repetition during games, so they can be in prime shape for a game, able to join the first string without losing a beat.

Coaches' checklist

The day before the game, a coach should be well prepared and organized in terms of having a roster, depth chart, and list of situation plays attached to a clipboard. A coach should stock his or her car with a ball bag, medical kit, water jug, and equipment box, all of which will be present on the sidelines during the game. A coach should get a good night's sleep and eat a well-balanced breakfast in the morning to start the day right. The last thing a coach needs is a stressful rush to a game as the result of disorganization or fatigue. The morning of the game should be a relaxing experience during which a coach can focus on the game plan and make the day enjoyable for his or her players.

Equipment check

The day before the game, make sure all your players' equipment is **functional** and in working order. Do not wait until game day to fuss around with equipment malfunctions. When equipment problems occur on game day, it lessens the team's concentration. The day of the game, players have to be organized, weighed, stretched, warmed up, and rehearsed on the offensive and defensive plays that will be executed during the game. Always be prepared for the worst. Have an equipment box handy, complete with mouthpieces (often forgotten), chin straps, helmet snaps, belts, and even an extra game jersey.

Game-day ritual

A coach should always write a short, detailed letter to parents informing them of their children's responsibilities for preparing for game day. Players are responsible for receiving field directions (handed out by coaches) during the week, reporting any equipment problems, laying out their uniform the night before, waking up at an appropriate time, and eating a balanced meal in the morning. This will give children the sort of discipline that fosters punctuality and preparation for any occasion, especially for a game. This ritual will also give parents a break from rushing to dress a child in the morning. Players will be less likely to misplace a piece of equipment. Parents should keep a list of phone numbers of other team parents, just in case they need to carpool or get more accurate directions to the game.

Parents can supervise their children in eating a well-balanced meal two hours before a game. If the game is early in the morning, kids should eat a small bowl of cereal with some fruit. Breakfast is the most important meal for a young football player. It should be a mix of all the food groups and give a player plenty of energy for the day's activities.

Pregame preparation will make the family drive to the game a relaxed one. No family wants the aggravation and hostility of being lost or late for a game. It makes for one awful experience, when the day should be an enjoyable one from start to finish.

Weight loss no-nos

All organized youth-football leagues have weight restrictions, especially for the skilled positions. Coaches should know the weight restrictions for every position. No coach should ever tell a child or parent that the child should lose a large amount of weight in order to play a desired position. Parents are often guilty of encouraging children to do so, and may resort to extreme measures, such as having their child fast and sweat down the pounds with rigorous workouts to make weight for game day.

Starving a young player's body of nutrients will ultimately decrease his or her performance. Young players who are not eating properly will become lethargic and moody. They will lack concentration during practices and games. Do not allow parents to endanger a child's long-term health. Children can get in the habit of missing meals or even develop eating disorders. Parents have to be patient and wait until their children hit the high-school level, where there are no weight restrictions. Then football players can challenge for any position, regardless of their weight.

Pregame jitters

A case of nerves often strikes young football players before a game. Kids frequently doubt their own ability to compete with their peers on the football field. They worry about their chances of fumbling the ball, catching the ball, missing a tackle, or missing a blocking assignment.

If a player is in doubt, they have already lost. Football players need confidence in themselves. That confidence needs to be established in practice sessions during the week. Parents should encourage their children to listen at practice, ask questions when in doubt, and study their playbook, so there is no confusion when they are at practice or when they are entering a game.

One of the many benefits of youth sports is that it establishes a good work ethic for players. Kids learn a valuable lesson: "If you study hard enough and know everything you need to know about a subject, there will be no reason to be nervous or doubt your ability."

Foundation for the future

Substituting young players in the game is a benefit to you in the long run. Most likely those subs coming off the bench are first-year players who can be potential starters for you next season. What a difference a year makes when you give those young players game experience. Keep in mind these kids are going to physically mature in height and weight just in time for next season. By giving your substitute players valuable playing time, you are building a foundation for the future. There is no better teacher than experience. Kids can get a taste of a real in-game situation. They will have the whole off-season to prepare themselves and realize the dedication it takes to compete with opposing players. Experience will build not only the players' confidence, but their parents' as well. All parents want to see their children make progress—and more important, be happy.

Never quit

In some games, your team will be physically overmatched in size or skill, and this may result in a substantial touchdown lead for your opponent. It's amazing to me how one touchdown can demoralize a young football team. In their view, the game is already over. When players give up easily, it really bothers me; it's another pitfall I'll have to prepare the team for in practice during the week.

It's always a good idea to teach the "never give up" scenario. Sometimes falling behind in a game can become a great learning experiences. The relaxed atmosphere will allow both teams to substitute players.

Teams tend to relax with a lead. Your players should take advantage of this by working doubly hard at their positions to swing the momentum into their favor. Next thing you know, your team will be mounting a comeback—perhaps one that takes your team all the way to victory.

I always use this motivational strategy to get my players going when they're down: I rate levels of intensity as A, B, and C. In a "C game," kids are not showing much effort and just look lethargic in their performance on the field. In a "B game," the team is playing at an average or below-average level. An "A game" features all-out effort and intense desire to achieve. When my players are down, I always give them this speech: "I've seen your B game. Now give me your A game. I know what you guys are capable of. Now show me on the field." Little speeches like this get the kids pumped up.

Filming your football games

It may seem a little extreme to film youth-football games, but it will produce the single most important learning tool for a coach to have.

Breaking down the game footage after a game allows you and your assistant coaches to evaluate players in a real competitive atmosphere. Films do not lie. Films will reveal which players are slacking and which are hard at work. A coach can view tapes to test new techniques or new play designs to see what works.

The most important part (probably by far) of filming games, especially for beginning coaches, is observing what other teams are successful at. There is no shame in copying other teams who are successful year after year. Some teams have developed a system, or they have a veteran coach who has found a way to consistently win at the youth level.

You're probably asking yourself who is going to film your games. An assistant coach can be your first choice. Then you can go down the line, asking parents to do the deed. You can even give parents a copy of the game on DVD as an incentive, so all the parents will have something to cherish.

Official ruling

Referees can be your best friends or your worst enemies. Always try to be respectful before, during, and after a game. I'm sure you'll get your share of bad calls, but I don't think officials are malicious toward any players unless the player is intentionally causing harm. Never indulge in a **negative outburst** toward a referee in front of your players. Your players may think this is appropriate behavior and may mimic your actions during a game.

Yes, sometimes players inform you of dirty play from the opposing team—holding, punches, late hits, and so on. Never confront the opposing players or coaches during a game. Get the referee's attention and tell him or her what to look out for. If the dirty play continues, call a time-out and discuss the matter with the referee and the opposing coach until matters are settled. Forbid your players from retaliating by fighting on the field. Say, "Just tell your coaches, and we will handle the situation."

Fans in the stands

You are always going to have some hecklers in the stands, be they friend or foe. It's a good idea to just ignore them. Interacting with fans will only escalate the situation into something negative. Show confidence in your stature. Show fans that no one can break your focus on the game with a few negative words. Concentrate on your play calling and on your players. If fans are really inappropriate in their language, find a league official or tell the field referee. Have the fan removed or stop the game before the situation gets out of control.

A good pregame tip is to always try to get the sideline farthest from the fans. This way you can separate yourself from hecklers, and your players won't find themselves interacting with parents until after the game is over.

Sometimes the disturbances in the stands come from your team's parents themselves. There are a lot of macho dads out there who want to share their opinions and give advice on how to coach. Meanwhile, they refuse to volunteer as coaches; they are only personal trainers to their own sons and daughters. Parents like this have a habit of undermining the coaches' teaching techniques, instilling their own tactics into the child instead. Doing this confuses the child, who isn't sure which person to listen to. These situations make coaching more difficult, because all your teachings can go right out the window.

Sideline behavior

Head coaches and assistant coaches should learn to control their emotions on the sidelines. Outbursts toward a player during the game can be embarrassing for you and the player. Instead call the player aside and tell them, "Remember what we practiced." That is the key. What you practice with your players during the week is what should be executed during the game. Many times it's the coach's fault for not practicing the nuances of the fundamentals that give players the tools to work with in a game. All your preparation should be done during the weeks leading up to the game. Game-day coaches should feel relaxed and confident that they prepared the players to the best of their ability. If foul-ups happen during the game, you don't take it out on the kids. You wait for the next practice to work on the mistakes, so they don't happen again.

If you are one of these rah-rah coaches who yells and screams at the entire team, then you are calling attention to yourself. Usually it will be in a negative light in the eyes of parents and fans. It's all right to be a cheerleader, but don't gloat and react in an "in your face" manner. Believe me, people respect a coach who gives off that confident vibe by just their mannerisms on the sidelines during the game.

The pressure to win

The pressure on kids to win becomes more extreme at the Midget level, especially for kids who have been playing football for a while. Winning gradually becomes more important to the players. As they get older, they mature in mind and body, and their priorities shift.

Older kids can develop a complex regarding winning and losing, and will grow restless if they're not winning games. Some frustrated players are likely to lose interest. If your team loses interest, it will be hard to motivate them to work harder.

Kids may fall under peer pressure from other teams in the league. As coaches we always want our players to believe in our teachings. We want the kids to know that all their effort in practice is not for nothing. Yes, there's the old saying, "Winning isn't everything," but you do need a few wins to build morale and keep kids interested in learning under your instruction. With a couple of wins, kids will continue to have interest and be productive—and more importantly, to respect you and have fun with you.

Ten

Advice for Parents

This chapter is a guide for parents on how to prepare their children for football. It's important to be active in your child's life. Parents serve as great role models while slowly breaking their child into sports. Here are some helpful hints on grooming your child for football.

When should a child start football?

It is very important to start football at a young age. Playing organized football at a young age allows your child to be in a structured football environment. They will develop the social skills and motor skills that come with playing football.

Football is a complex sport; it is always evolving with new terms and techniques. In football, knowledge is power, and so is experience. So it's important for kids to start young, so they can gain as much experience and knowledge as possible. I've seen many young kids become superstars just because they know how the game is to be played. They have no fear and are confident in their skills.

Many parents nowadays are preventing their children from participating until high school. Players who join up for the first time at this age are far behind their counterparts who have been playing since grade school. These newcomers fall behind, get discouraged, and are more likely to quit. Who knows what their potential could have been if they had started young?

What about the hits?

It's important to learn the basics and fundamentals of football, but it's just as important to learn how to fall and absorb collisions. The best time to learn is at the Pee Wee level, where collisions are mild. Kids will learn the techniques of giving and receiving contact. Young football players can adapt their bodies to absorbing contact and make split-second decisions to avoid collisions altogether.

Keep in mind that contact and collisions intensify through each level of football, from Pee Wee, to Midget, to high school, to college, and to the NFL level. Children grow with the sport each year in physical size, strength, and speed. The bigger and faster the kids get, the more violent the collisions become. Football training in a child's early years will physically and mentally prepare them for contact.

Choosing the right sport

Football is not for every child. What you see on television is the glamour of the sport. What you don't see is the hard work and preparation that takes place before the game. Some kids are under the assumption that when they join the local football team, it's going to be like television, with a lot of passing and frequent touchdowns. In reality, football takes a lot of conditioning and preparation. This may discourage kids from participating, because they don't see the reward as worth the effort.

A parent cannot force a child to like a sport. A child must find something he or she can get out of it. Most often children value the game as fun, challenging, and inspiring to their self-esteem. A parent can save a lot of money and distress by evaluating early on whether the child enjoys the sport. It would be good idea to try a variety of sports, so the child has options to compare. Whatever sport your child chooses, make sure you support his or her decision.

Medical clearance

Before any child participates in organized sports, they need to receive a clear bill of health from a doctor at a mandatory physical. A **full physical** will detect any health concerns that might interfere with a child's athletic career. At a young age, children can develop high blood pressure, diabetes, asthma, allergies, heart murmurs, and even the enlargement of the heart that has been common in athletes.

Clearly the most rapidly growing problem for young football players is weight gain. More and more kids are becoming overweight and inactive. A diet of fast food cannot be expected to fuel a young athlete's body for practices or games.

Before- and after-practice meals

For young players to perform at their best on the football field, they need to learn to eat a well-balanced diet, which will help them build strength, recover from injuries, and maintain long-term energy. **Complex carbohydrates** are good sources of lasting energy. Simple carbohydrates (like candy) give the body only a sudden boost of energy, not the prolonged periods of energy that complex carbohydrates do.

Proteins are the building blocks repairing muscle tissue that has been stressed by rigorous practices. Proteins contain amino acids that can repair muscle fibers and speed up the healing process for injured players.

The next time you go grocery shopping, make sure you pick up some whole-wheat breads, wild rice, brown rice, or oatmeal cereals to give your player a carbohydrate power boost before a practice. Then grab some protein-rich items, like milk, eggs, chicken, fish, and yogurt for after-practice muscle repair.

If it's tough to get your athlete to eat properly, maybe it's time to make a change for the entire family. Begin by buying and eating more healthful foods. Then Mom and Dad can be active in eating right and being physically active, which will influence the children to do the same.

Teaching the basics

It is important for all parents to read as many books and view as many instructional videos on football as possible. Even if you were a star athlete in your day, it's a good idea to brush up on old material and learn the new techniques coaches are using around the country.

For example, I was an outstanding running back in my day, but I have no business teaching other positions I know little about. I would be doing an injustice to my players if I taught them the wrong way. In other words, don't teach something you know nothing about. Yes, I know every father wants to be macho and demonstrate the different positions on the football field. That's great! But such dads need to make sure they did their homework first.

I suggest taking your child to some high-school or college practices to observe the different fundamentals applied to each position. You can even go online and type in "instructional football videos," and a variety of Web sites catering to football will pop up.

Being active with your child

Children will benefit greatly from parents who are actively involved in their learning. Teach and demonstrate by example. Children learn most efficiently by watching, then mimicking the activity. Explaining with words will sometimes have kids confused, because they have never experienced what you are explaining to them. When you demonstrate skills, your player will get the concept you're trying to get across. Being active also makes your time together fun, because you're running around and being playful.

There are lots of ways to practice with your child. Besides running-pass patterns, you can do an array of conditioning drills. How about push-ups or sprints? A parent's enthusiasm for football will translate into a child's interest in football. Your child will look up to you as a role model and will appreciate your efforts down the road.

Teaching your child to be a complete football player

A child should learn **every position** on the football field, from offensive guard to cornerback—no matter their size or weight. It's good for young beginners to have an appreciation even for skills they are unlikely to use immediately, such as punting and kicking. It is very common for a child to play numerous positions as he or she grows in age and physical size. A child could start out as a lineman at the Pee Wee level, then later grow enough to become a running back at the Midget level.

Realistic expectations

It is very important that you don't groom a player into the position you want the child play. You have to be realistic about setting goals. Physically your child may not have the speed to play running back, or the hands to be a receiver—at least not at his or her current age.

Youth football is the time to groom your child for success. Have your child learn all the positions on the football field. Every position can be made into a personal challenge for a child. Keep in mind that versatile football players can be extremely valuable to high-school or college coaches in future years. For now encourage your child and build his or her self-esteem, no matter what position your child plays. In the end, he or she will be a well-rounded player.

Parental patience

When you're teaching your child or doing some drills with them, don't become frustrated if he or she doesn't pick something up quickly. If you flare up, you will only create a stressful environment. Pressure on a child causes emotional stress.

That emotional stress causes muscle tension that will physically affect performance on a football field. A parent must be positive and encouraging. Carrying on in a hostile manner will put your child on edge. He or she will be afraid to make mistakes—and will most likely lose confidence. Remember, these are young children. All children play better when they are loose, relaxed, and confident.

Do not let frustration build up to the point that you say something you'll regret later on. The goal for these young children is to gain experience. You want a child to make mistakes. They'll learn from them. A good motto to remember is that "repetition is the mother of all skill."

Positive praise

Children love praise and attention. There is no acceptance more important to children than their parents'. Words from someone they admire go a long way in building children's character. Positive reinforcement is the main building block in success at anything a child may do. Let's face it: it's easy to dwell on the bad things that happen, because they seem to happen so often in our lives.

Even when a child makes mistakes, there is always something a parent can say that will uplift him or her. Positive words and gestures can be so powerful; use them as much as possible in regards to your child's performance: "You made a nice catch out there." "You are getting better and better at this game." "Keep working hard, and good things will happen."

Practice in open fields

If you are an active parent who wants to work on your child's skills, I recommend that you go to a football field or a big open park. The reason for this is to change the atmosphere into a football environment. At home there are too many distractions. Injuries can happen, and boredom can set in from playing in confined areas. Going to an open field brings excitement. A big, open field makes a child feel as if they are in a real football practice or a game.

You can do an array of conditioning drills with your child in an open field. You can throw, run, and catch in open areas. Best of all, you are in a playful atmosphere with no worries, away from the everyday stresses of the world. You can just enjoy each other's company.

Making time in your busy schedule

The sheer number of parental no-shows at games baffles me. It's as if games and practices are a babysitting service where parents can just drop off their children and go on their merry way. You don't know how many times a player—especially an unsung player—will make a great play, with no one in the stands to share it with. It is heartbreaking!

Attention and approval from parents is the strongest reward a child can receive. I do understand that parents work and have busy lives, but telling your child "I heard you did great in the game" is not good enough. Parents have to make an effort to show their children that they care and are proud of their children's achievements. Make some time to see your children's games. Your most important job in life is being a parent. Make appointments and change your schedules around your child's games.

Listening as a bonding tool

Many kids, especially first-year players, will have questions or doubts about playing football. It's important that parents have a good, open relationship with their children. You would never want your child to feel that he or she can't come to you with questions or problems. If you have a history of criticizing or critiquing, your child will probably not come to you for help. The fear of a negative response will only discourage the child more. For some children, facing a problem alone can be all right. For others, it is not. Many children who cannot face their problems become quiet and unproductive.

Parents always have to be the **support group** for their children. Parents sometimes show more respect to the child's teammates than they do their own children. Leave some time in your busy day to talk. Take care of any other distractions or preoccupations, so you can focus on your child's issues. Find some time to be alone by going to the movies or going for a walk in a park. Always be positive, and give good advice when your child comes to you with a problem.

Teammate bonding

Parents can make the football experience a special one for the entire team. Parents can arrange small parties for players' birthdays, pregame meals, and even after-game celebrations, no matter if the team wins or loses. The team can bond in a fun atmosphere, no matter how old they are or which schools they attend outside of football. Let the players enjoy each other's company and make the football experience a memorable one. Parties can also bring the families together and make for a great cheering section in the stands on game day.

Socially, football is a great way for shy kids to make new friends. Working hard all week at practice and sacrificing their bodies for the benefit of the team during games tends to bring football players together.

If your child gets hurt

By all means, if your child gets hurt in practice or at home, **don't remove them from the football environment**. He or she can still go to practice and even get involved in helping the coach do drills. The child can probably learn something just by observing and running a few drills. Being away from practice due to injury may cause the child to pursue other activities. They may also forget the knowledge they worked so hard for. You don't want a child to fall behind in learning. By observing at practice, a child will develop a desire to get back on the football field.

Lack of playing time

It is tough to keep your composure when your child is not in the game. Before you explode in rage, ask yourself a couple of questions.

1. Has my child missed a practice?
2. Is my child goofing off in practice?
3. Is my child a first-year player, learning the game?
4. Is my child giving effort in practice?
5. Does my child lack confidence?

The answers may explain why your child is not playing. The logical step is to confront the coach in a respectful way. I'm sure he or she can give you a direct reason why your child is seeing limited playing time. Never be confrontational with a coach. The best way to obtain answers to your questions is to attend practices. I always loved it when parents came to practice. At practice, parents can gauge their child's progress and skill level compared with the rest of the team. Attending practice can stop you from making a rush to judgment that you may regret.

Extra protective accessories

Extra protective accessories are always good for a young football player to have. Kids are always going to get nicked, scratched, cut, kicked, and stepped on. Popular football gloves are great for ball handling, but they are also good for protecting a child's knuckles and fingers from being harmed during blocking and tackling. Elbow pads serve as a good buffer for close-quarter blocking situations and will also prevent scrapes when your child hits the turf. Even long socks can shield children from the shin kicks that can happen in a practice or game.

The items above and other protective gear will help prevent any distractions that interfere with a player's performance. Remember, any cut or scratch is a big deal at this age. Their entire focus changes, and their production may be slowed or even halted.

It is amazing to me how often I have to ask my players to ask their parents to buy them some accessories for protection. Practice after practice, there would be no sign of any new protective gear. Some parents will just not make time to go to the sports store for a fifteen-dollar purchase.

Besides publishing a book, I'm also in the process of designing my own line of safety equipment that will help protect young football players. With all of my field experience, I'm familiar with the types of injuries players are susceptible to. With a little creativity and some luck, this small-time coach is looking to make a big difference in parents' and children's lives.

Becoming a team booster

Being a team booster allows you to support your child's team for the season and for generations to come. Booster clubs raise money through fund-raisers such as bake sales, T-shirts, mugs, and raffle giveaways. Funds generated can go toward new football equipment, uniforms, trophies, and even to the end-of-the-year award ceremonies. Donating your time builds your youth program for the benefit of the children in the community.

Parents sometimes take the youth athletic programs in this country for granted. Many countries have no youth athletic programs at all for their children. Children in these countries lose out on developing work ethic, discipline, and social skills; they may lack the structure in their lives that sports can provide. With so much time on their hands, these children may find time to hang around in the streets, getting involved in drugs and possibly causing mischief in their communities. Take advantage of the society we live in. Support your local youth team even when your child has moved on. You will help shape our children's lives for generations to come.

Making winning easy

It's important that parents teach children that a game victory isn't the only success to be found in football. **Success** can be any little thing that makes us happy or a memory that we can remember for a lifetime. Little achievements in practice, like making a great tackle, represent success. Making friends with teammates represents success as well.

It's always easy to think about the negatives that happen in our lives. Kids are especially hard on themselves, because of the peer pressure from others. We tend to compare ourselves to others who are having success. Everyone has a different definition of success. As a parent, you can teach your children to cherish the little successes that happen in their lives. When parents praise little successes, children will broaden their idea of success.

Teach children that winning is simple to achieve—and there is more than one way to win. Winning can be doing a drill better than anyone else. Winning can be making the starting team. Whenever a child can build self-esteem, it's a victory. Winning can be simple to recognize if we open our eyes to the little successes that can happen in a practice or a game.

Extra Points: Football Fitness

When can a child begin lifting weights? According to recent studies by Dr. Avery Faigenbaum, properly supervised strength training can improve strength and body composition, increase cardiorespiratory fitness, increase flexibility, improve motor skills, increase resistance to injury, and enhance mental health and well-being.

Although there is no recommended minimum age for strength training, it is important for a child to be emotionally mature. Kids must be able to understand instructions and use proper technique. It is also important that a child perform an exercise program specifically designed for them. A parent, coach, or supervisor cannot whip out an old bodybuilding program or college workout and expect a child to participate in it. Bodybuilding and hoisting large amount of weights should not be the goal for a young football player. A child's body is not mature enough to heave heavy loads! Older players should be encouraged to lift heavy weights that will give them a suit of armor to protect them from harm. I believe lifting weights will only hurt a child. It will give them an ego boost, but they really should be focused on improving overall strength, flexibility, and endurance. I personally recommend doing light weight exercises that will improve the overall core of the body. Strength exercises with a person's own body weight or even resistance bands can improve motor skills, balance, and coordination, which should be the real focus for young athletes starting their football careers.

A **calisthenic program** can be sufficient to develop strength. I suggest exercises that are specific to football; for instance, blocking and tackling utilizes a lot of chest, arm, and shoulder action. I suggest having your child perform sets of ten to fifteen push-ups. Then progress to more reps as he or she gets stronger. Standing squats (with no weight added) is another good exercise, because it develops leg strength. Running short sprints and hills is an excellent full-body workout. Jumping rope can improve balance and speed. Are you starting to get the idea?

Be careful, warm up, and stretch before you start any activity.

Stretching for speed, power, and coordination

Stretching is a great activity for kids to get into. Young athletes should learn about the functions, motions, and limits of each body part. Stretching is an important part of sports participation. Limber muscles and ligaments yield superior coordination, strength, and speed. More importantly, stretching can prevent injuries and reduce muscle soreness after a tough practice. Stretching sessions can also be a time to relax and focus on the objectives for the day. Flexibility can be the best preparation ritual children can learn at the beginning of their sports careers.

Some of the basics of stretching are as follows: Warm up properly with fifteen to twenty minutes of light aerobic activity, such as jogging. The warming-up process allows blood flow through the muscles of the body, which will allow muscles to be limber during stretching. Stretching cold muscles can cause muscle and ligament tears that may take weeks to heal. Add a relaxed yoga vibe by breathing slowly, so tension doesn't interrupt your stretch. Keep muscles relaxed and hold each stretch for thirty seconds.

Lifestyle and eating habits

It's relatively easy to get kids to eat healthfully when they're young. It's even easier if a parent serves as a role model in choosing healthy snacks and meals. High-calorie diets of junk food can drain energy levels. Extra weight can make the heart work much harder. The old saying, "They're young, they'll burn it off," shouldn't exist anymore. Children watch television more than ever these days. The advent of video game consoles such as PlayStation and Xbox has worsened the problem as well. Surfing the Internet for hours is another ingredient for inactive children.

Little changes such as avoiding caffeinated and sugary drinks are a good start. Caffeine combined with not drinking enough water can lead to heat stroke and muscle cramps on the football field. Stick with water to quench thirst.

Get your children to eat more fruits and vegetables for energy and the recovery of sore muscles. Fruits and vegetables contain a high concentration of **electrolytes**, which are lost through sweating. Inadequate amounts of electrolytes cause a shortage of blood flow to the muscles, which causes painful muscle cramps.

Remember, children look up to their parents. You don't have to preach to them about eating well. Children can learn by example.

Final Thoughts

It wasn't hard to write this book. A matter of fact, I felt I was obligated to express my feelings about my experiences in youth football. As a coach without a child of my own on the team, I'm in the minority. I can view youth football in an unbiased way.

I've seen many teams lose their unity because of the animosity between parents. I've seen coaches holler at kids as if they were dogs. I've witnessed fans cursing at referees for the most minor of offenses. People are sometimes just out of control when it comes to their children. This "win at all costs" mentality is ridiculous. Parents cheer and complain as if their child were going to sign a million-dollar contract next year.

Whatever you witness as a coach should not discourage you from coaching football. Focus on your kids. Give them attention and guidance, and you'll be just fine. Be the glue that keeps the community together by always keeping parents informed with newsletters or phone calls on events, meetings, and schedule changes. Also keep in contact with parents whose children are behind in grasping the concepts of football. Give them some feedback on what can make their child's football experience better.

Be creative in your coaching philosophy. Use the ideas in this book and supplement them with your own. What you put into coaching is what you'll get out of it. Have a cutting-edge when it comes to preparing, communicating, and creating techniques to inspire your players to give their best performance.

Above all, have fun … and make coaching football the best experience you ever had.

Special thanks to Jessie Tateo, Daniel Tateo, Jack DiPietro, Jamie Scaglione, and Brian Ferguson for their support and dedication to youth football.

Bibliography

Gavin, Mary L., MD; Steven A. Dowshen, MD; and Neil Izenberg, MD. *KidsHealth. New York*, 2004, pp. 34–35, 153, 182–84.

American Fitness Professionals & Associates. AFPA Certification Manual. New Jersey, 2003, pp. 80, 97, 296.

Foran, Bill. *High performance sports conditioning*. Champaign, IL: Human Kinetics, 2001, pp. 87–97, 237–40.

Ball, Stephen D. "Weight Lifting and Kids." http://www.missourifamilies.org/features/nutritionarticles/fit.htm (viewed 11/27/2005)

KidsHealth. "Dehydration." 2006. http://kidshealth.org/firstaid-safe/emergencies/dehydration.html

Mac, Brian. "Hill Training." 2006. http://brainmac.demon.co/uk/hilltrain.htm#web

American Council on Exercise. "ACE Fit Facts." 1999. http://acefitness.org/fitfacts/ff/39.html

Gavin, Mary L. M.D., Steven A. Dowshen M.D., Neil Izenberg, M.D. FitKids, New York, 2004. pp. 182-184

Gavin, Mary L. Steven A. Dowshen M.D., Neil Izenberg, M.D., Fitkids, New York, 2004. pp. 34-35

Gavin, Mary L. M.D., Steven A. Dowshen M.D., Neil Izenberg, Fitkids, New York, 2004, p.153

American Fitness & Associates, AFPA Certification Manual, New Jersey, 2003, p.80

American Fitness & Associates, AFPA Certification Manual, New Jersey, 2003, p. 97

American Fitness & Associates, AFPA Certifaication Manual, New Jersey, 2003, p. 296

Foran, Bill (2001), High Performance Sports Conditioning, Champaign, IL: Human Kinetics, pp. 87-97

Foran, Bill (2001), High Performance Sports Conditioning, Champaign, IL: Human Kinetics, pp. 237-240

Mac, Brian (2000) Hill training, http://brianmac.demon.co.uk. hilltrain.htm#web

American Council on Exercise, 1999, ACE Fit Facts, http://Acefitness. org/Fitfacts/ff/39.html

978-0-595-40246-5
0-595-40246-1